NARROW BOATS
Ownership, Care and Maintenance

NARROW BOATS
Ownership, Care and Maintenance

MICHAEL STIMPSON

THE CROWOOD PRESS

First published in 2019 by
The Crowood Press Ltd
Ramsbury, Marlborough
Wiltshire SN8 2HR

www.crowood.com

© Michael Stimpson 2019

All rights reserved. No part of this publication may be reproduced or transmitted in any form or by any means, electronic or mechanical, including photocopy, recording, or any information storage and retrieval system, without permission in writing from the publishers.

British Library Cataloguing-in-Publication Data
A catalogue record for this book is available from the British Library.

ISBN 978 1 78500 551 0

Typeset by Jean Cussons Typesetting, Diss, Norfolk

Printed and bound in India by Parksons Graphics

CONTENTS

Preface   6
Introduction   7

1.	Narrow Boat History	11
2.	Types of Craft	16
3.	Craft Uses	29
4.	The Inland Waterways	34
5.	Buying a Narrow Boat	42
6.	Running Costs	49
7.	Decoration	57
8.	Waterworks	62
9.	Equipment	65
10.	Electrics	72
11.	Engines	75
12.	When Things Go Wrong	83
13.	Responsible Boating	91
14.	Going Further	101

Glossary   105
Index   159

PREFACE

Much of this work is based on my own forty years' experience of owning a boat, but I have also drawn on surveys of other craft in my line of work. It is intended to be a 'dipping in' book; a prospective narrow boat owner may well want to read it from start to finish but some information is repeated where the subject fits the chapter.

Cruising the inland waterways is a tranquil way to spend your leisure time. There are thousands of miles of canal and river to explore and enjoy, and wayside inns to visit at the end of your boating day.

The average use of a narrow boat is two to three weeks and six to eight weekends a year, but there are many owners who cruise more extensively. Some couples share a boat and take it in turns to use her.

Some boat owners get up early and boat all day whilst others will boat for a few hours and tie up to undertake work on their boat, talk to other boat owners or explore the local area that they find themselves in.

Many canal-based events take place around the system throughout the year, from rallies to smaller events. Many of these are organized by the Inland Waterways Association, others by local boat clubs who want to introduce the joys of the waterways to local folk in their area.

I would like to thank my friends Trevor Whitling and Hugh Mcknight for reading early drafts of this book and offering constructive comments, which have been incorporated in the final work, and to Sue Cawson for reading the whole text before I submitted it to the publishers.

Most of the photos in this book are from my own collection, but about three dozen have kindly been donated by friends, some taken specifically for this book. My thanks go to them for their help.

I hope the reader enjoys it.

Michael Stimpson, Rickmansworth
January 2019

INTRODUCTION

Buying a boat is not an investment. It is unlikely to increase in value – over the years, it will either maintain or lose its value. This depends on the level of maintenance the craft has received during its life. 'A boat is a hole in the water into which one throws money!'

One aspect of boating that has grown out of all proportion over the last fifty years is the bulk of craft being used on our massive inland waterways network. The design of these craft is based on the original narrow boats that were the mainstay of the goods-carrying fleets that used to move cargos round the country. While there are still a good number of ex-working narrow boats around, recent years have seen a vast expansion of modern craft to fill the need for leisure use and floating homes. Boatyards all over this country and abroad have been producing hulls and the numbers of these craft have grown at a steady rate.

If you want to buy a boat that can cruise the majority of the inland waterways network in the UK then it is likely to be a narrow boat. If you want to cover all the inland non-tidal system then the maximum size is 57ft 6in long by 6ft 10in beam (17.5m × 2m).

A pair of narrow boats carrying coal on the Grand Union Canal. The rear boat (the butty) is travelling close up behind the motor boat and is connected with cross straps. Normal practice if the boats were loaded would be to have the butty on a long line.

The network we have today is somewhat smaller than we had 100 years ago, as many canals built to feed the Industrial Revolution have been closed and, in many cases, man or nature has wiped the line of the canal from the map. Some of these are now being rebuilt to provide even more waterway routes for us all to enjoy and much of the UK is still connected by inland waterways; for example, you can take a narrow boat from London to Manchester or from Gloucester to York with ease.

Before the decline of the network of canals in the 1960s the main use of the system was for the transport of goods. With the passing of this era the network started to fall into decline. The rivers of course were natural and thus kept flowing, but the canals started to fall into disuse and thus into disrepair. As explored later in this book, the system was revived by the hard work of volunteers, and the main use of the network today is leisure.

Why would such a collection of connected waterways become so popular? Perhaps each person using the system today would give a different answer but high on the list would be the peace and tranquillity out on the water.

There are three types of waterway:

Rivers, which are, of course, natural and were either used as they were or improved by man-made locks and weirs to aid navigation

Navigations, which are artificial waterways that divert and/or shorten the course of a river but which get their supply of water from the connected river

Canals, which are totally man-made and which, in the main, were built as a method of transporting goods during the Industrial Revolution.

Without the Industrial Revolution there would not have been the need for the large network of canals, yet without the canals the Industrial Revolution may not have happened – this may sound like a paradox and indeed it is. One wonders if the Industrial Revolution would have happened the way it did, or at all, if a method of getting raw materials to the new factories and finished goods away, cheaply and in quantity, had not been found. The cost of goods to the end user went down dramatically and, as it was seen how beneficial a network of waterways would be, more and more canals were built in a rush known as 'Canal Mania', and many canals, some of which did not see the light of day, were promoted. The same thing, of course, happened with the railways a century later.

Other benefits of transport by water as opposed to pack horse or cart were the amount of goods that could be transported in one load and the lower risk of damage to finished products.

Early canals were contour canals that hugged the lie of the land, but later canals took a more direct route from A to B, using tunnels, embankments and aqueducts to maintain the level. These were harder to build but cut down the journey time. There are a number of locations where a canal route winds round a point on the route for hours because the canal was built on a level and thus took the longer way round by keeping to the contour of the land.

Like the later railways, the canal system was built to a number of different sizes, but unlike the railways, which eventually were standardized on 4ft 8½in (1.4m), canals are still separated by the different sizes that were used to determine the size of the locks and thus the size and type of craft that could fit into them.

The canals of the south are mainly barge canals, which have locks that can take craft 72ft (22m) long and 14ft (4.3m) beam. The northern canals were built to the same beam but were shorter, at either 62ft (18.9m) or 57ft (17.4m). Most canals were built to the Midland narrow boat size of 71ft 6in (21.8m) by 7ft (2.1m) beam. If you have a full-length narrow boat then you are not able to navigate some of the northern canals, as the craft are too long for the locks. A short boat on the northern canals cannot get through the Midlands, as the locks here are not wide enough. Only the canals of the south can take both types of craft, with some of the locks being built to take barges, while others were widened to enable a pair of narrow boats to fit side by side.

INTRODUCTION

A boat horse at rest. This is a shire but other breeds of heavy horse were sometimes used, particularly on canals where shires were too large.

All canals were built to move goods round the country and the craft used were open. On narrow boats, goods were protected from the elements only by sheets covering the hold, supported by a top plank sitting on masts in the centre of the craft. Barges had covers over the hold.

All craft were originally towed by a horse, although two donkeys or a team of men were also used in some cases. This use of a horse or a pair of donkeys resulted in a number of overnight stopping points springing up with stable facilities, adding to the enchanting buildings which can still be found around the waterway system.

In the mid-1800s, steam engines were built into narrow boats, although the steam plant boiler and fuel took up much-needed cargo space. Steam tugs were used to better effect to tow craft through tunnels and along long stretches of lock-free waterway. In the early 1900s, diesel engines were used to power craft, and as such units improved in reliability, more and more craft were retrofitted with them or new craft were built with them. This was one reason why so many working narrow boats were built in the 1930s, although there are still a number of boats built in the 1800s on the system today.

It was soon clear that a narrow boat with an engine had enough power to move itself complete with cargo and tow another loaded boat, so it became standard practice for a motor boat to be paired with a butty (friend or mate) boat. At first these were old horse-drawn boats, but they were gradually replaced by purpose-built butties. Horse boats had been used in pairs before the introduction of boat engines.

In the 1930s and 40s a motor boat and butty were often built in pairs for the same company (though not always at the same yard) and many spent their working life together. This practice carried on until the 1960s with the Admiral-class boats.

Working craft were built to take knocks and to have bulk cargo loaded into them. Most current owners of such craft take a pride in and look after them as historic items as well as to maintain their value. You do not buy an ex-working narrow boat

– rather you pay a sum of money to become its curator for a number of years.

Original narrow boats were built of wood, with oak sides and elm bottoms. Later on, iron and steel replaced the oak sides but the elm bottoms were kept (in vessels known as composite craft) until finally all-iron or steel boats were the norm.

During World War II, a few concrete narrow boats (and other types of craft) were built to provide a quick way of supplying additional craft for transporting food, munitions and other goods throughout the country, but these were a short-term solution as concrete is not a good product for hull production. Today, only steel is used and the modern boat has a weed hatch built into the stern, which allows access to the propeller so any item caught round the propeller can be cleared. Older craft did not have this.

If a craft has a weed hatch then it is a good idea to have a watertight bulkhead forward of the engine room, as this will prevent the craft from sinking in the event of water coming in through the weed hatch, the stern tube or any outlets in the hull (for raw water intakes, engine cooling and so on). Sadly, a high percentage of craft are built without such protection and a high percentage of sinkings are caused by this omission.

The bulk of narrow boats and other types of craft nowadays are for private pleasure use, although the number of residential craft is on the rise and there are also a large number of craft still used for commercial activity in many different forms – hire craft, hotel boats, passenger trip boats, day hire craft, cargo carriers, maintenance craft and floating shops, both static and mobile. Commercial use of the waterways in its many forms is alive, well and thriving.

While the original use of the canal system is, in the main, no longer with us there are still boats carrying bulk cargo, as this can still be an economical way to transport goods. Where the goods are not perishable and the run is either short or there are not too many locks in the way, a conveyor belt-type system can be provided.

Most people first discover the enchanting world of the inland waterways on foot. I know I did in the mid-1960s. The urban waterside environment includes buildings and structures built over 200 years ago that provide a glimpse back into our past. Whilst in some cases, such as Gas Street in Birmingham, this world has now been opened up to the rest of the environment, there are still places where you can feel you are back in the past. The countryside takes you to a peaceful and tranquil world away from the rush of the modern world of A roads and motorways, where you plod along at a sedate 4mph, seeing the wildlife that has made the canal or the banks its home.

CHAPTER 1

NARROW BOAT HISTORY

First of all, is it a narrow boat or a narrowboat? While many believe one word is acceptable, the majority view is that the correct way to describe a boat that is narrow is two words. Another interesting idea is that a narrow boat was built prior to 1950 and was used to carry goods, while a narrowboat is a modern craft also known as a steel canal cruiser. I will not enter this debate but in this book I will stick to narrow boat.

Traditionally a narrow boat was about 71ft 6in long by 7ft beam (21.8m by 2.1m) and was designed to fit into the locks of the Midland canal system, which developed as part of the early Industrial Revolution. They were designed for the carriage of cargo and

In the early days, the main motive power on the canal system was horses, and thus the system is covered with buildings that started life as stables, like this one on the Shropshire Union Canal.

could take up to 30 tons of goods drawn along by either one horse or two donkeys or mules. While the hull was mostly designed to carry cargo, there were a number of long-distance craft that had a cabin for the crew at the stern.

To cater for the horses and donkeys, there were a number of stables along the system, which have now either disappeared or been converted into other uses.

In the days of horse boats, the cabin was situated at the stern of the boat just forward of the steering position. When engines started being installed, the engine room was fitted forward of the back cabin. This resulted in a very long propeller (or prop) shaft but allowed the steerer access to the cramped living cabin at the back of the boat. As many horse boats were converted to motor boats, it was easier to instal the engine in the cargo hold forward of the back cabin, and this tradition was carried forward to new builds (boats built as motor narrow boats rather than being converted), so, despite the inconvenience of a long prop shaft running under the living area, the layout was not altered until modern leisure craft were introduced. The rear profile of the boat

A pair of GU boats in GUCC livery breasted up showing the mop sticks (mops) resting on the Buckby cans (water containers) on the roof of the back cabin. Note the three brass rings and the horse brasses on the chimneys. The butty boat has the back doors traditionally painted but the motor boat doors are plain. The photo also shows the fenders, which are positioned to prevent the rudder being caught in the mitre of the lock gates. The butty tiller has been removed to allow easy access to the back cabin. It was normal to turn the tiller round to have it pointing upwards.

A pair of FMC (Fellows, Morton and Clayton) boats attending the Rickmansworth Waterways Festival. The top planks are down rather than running along the top of the masts, which could then act as a support. Note the forward cabin on the butty.

needed to be altered for water to flow through the propeller. The cruiser stern allowed the engine to be installed under the back decks, which enabled the rest of the hull to be used for accommodation.

The first self-propelled craft were fitted with steam engines, but the loss of cargo space to the engine itself, the boiler and the stock of coal resulted in a continued hunt for some method of propulsion which took up less space. A Swedish firm (Bolinder) produced a single-cylinder 'heavy oil' engine that met the requirement and a number of 9hp and 13hp units were fitted to craft, resulting in the motor boat of today. Other companies also built single-cylinder heavy oil engines. Later, 18hp engines were used and then twin-cylinder units were introduced.

At first, narrow boats were owned or operated by the 'No 1s' – these boats were single craft and operated by the owner (or lessor), in later years often with the help of his family, who lived in the back cabins of the motor and butty boats. Later, the boats were owned by major canal carrying companies such as the Grand Union Canal Carrying Company (who owned 340 boats), the Shropshire Union R & C Co. and Fellows, Morton and Clayton. There were also numerous small fleets, such as Cadbury and Ovaltine, and at least two railway companies (London Midland and Scottish and Great Western) owned a number of craft.

The canal companies would charge tolls on craft that used their waterways and this was achieved by

The cratch board or deck board of a narrow boat is shaped to follow the contour of the side cloths (tarpaulins). It helped to prevent water from entering the hold when working up a lock, and also provided a useful support for the tunnel lamp, although this was often set on a separate stand in front of the cratch board.

'gauging' the boat, usually in a lock. A register was kept of boats with records of the gauging depth of the craft – that is, how deep in the water the craft would be for each ton of cargo.

A motor boat had enough power to tow another fully loaded boat so horse boats were paired up with motor boats to provide a total carrying capacity of 55 tons – 25 on the motor and 30 on the horse boat. Later specific 'butty' (friend or mate) boats were constructed to work in tandem with the motor boats.

While a number of ex-working boats were built earlier and some later, the bulk of the traditional craft now on the canal system were built in the 1930s for FMC (Fellows, Morton and Clayton) and the GUCCC (Grand Union Canal Carrying Company) to supplement the earlier craft owned and operating in both fleets. Many are still in working condition and some are still in commercial carrying use. Others have been converted by adding a superstructure and are used for both private pleasure and residential use. Having said that, there are still a good number of boats on the system today built in the 1800s.

In the 1960s, the traffic on our canal network was declining and large numbers of the working boat fleet were laid up out of use, although the last series of boats, the Admiral class, were built for the British Waterways Board in the 60s. Many were sunk, having had engines removed, in basins or 'flashes' to extend their life in case they were required again. A few enthusiasts tried to continue carrying, and one or two traffic runs, such as the lime juice from Brentford to Boxmoor (Willow Wren and Three Fellows Carrying and later T & D Murrell), did manage to carry on but, in the main, companies who had used the canals for the conveyance of goods turned to road vehicles instead. Our railway system suffered the same fate, as loading a lorry to take goods from door to door seemed at the time to be much more efficient, and in some ways it was.

Many believe that it was the railways that caused the death of canal-borne transport and, indeed, an effect was felt, but what the railways really did was change the way the canals were used. As an example, in Birmingham the short-haul traffic from the rail/canal interchange to the factories on the canal network in and around Birmingham increased. It was long-haul traffic that suffered.

It is true that some waterways did suffer from competition from the railways but others benefitted, such as in the Birmingham area, although even here some routes were lost.

A large number of ex-working boats have been cut down from 71ft 6in (21.8m), many to 60ft (18.3m) or 57ft 6in (17.5m) to enable them to navigate the northern canals (*see below*). Many were cut down and turned into tugs or ice breakers. There are even examples of craft having been shortened and then lengthened again!

A number of craft were cut in half, with a new bow being fitted to the stern half and a new counter being added to the bow, producing two 40–45ft (12.2–13.7m) boats. In some cases both halves claimed to be the original boat!

Early boats were built of wood – normally with oak sides and elm bottoms. Iron sides with elm bottoms and iron hulls were tried but steel hulls became the norm from the 1930s onwards, although some builders still constructed narrow boats from wood – Walker Brothers of Rickmansworth, for example, built both motor and butty boats for a number of companies, including the Grand Union Canal Carrying Company.

The design of the boats changed little, with the small living cabin at the stern then forward of the engine room on motor boats, which required a very long prop shaft running under the back cabin. The rest of the boat was given over to cargo. There were two stands and a mast in the hold to support the top plank, which ran from a block on the cabin roof at the back to the cratch board at the bow. The cratch (or deck) board was a triangular board at the bow that served to support the top plank and to prevent water entering the hold in such situations as a lock overflowing onto the bow.

Boat decoration will be dealt with in Chapter 7. Suffice to say here, the traditional style of narrow boat decoration still lives on today, with a high percentage of craft adhering to it.

While there are still many narrow boats constructed in the 1800s on the system today, the bulk of ex- working boats were built in the early 1900s, when canal carrying companies both replaced older craft and expanded the fleets of boats they owned. The best example is the Grand Union Canal Carrying Company, who in the early 1930s had three boatyards build the Star class and then the larger Town class fleets to augment the existing Royalty class, which came from Associated Canal Carriers when the GUCCC was formed.

CHAPTER 2

TYPES OF CRAFT

NARROW BOAT OWNERSHIP

Owning a narrow boat is a commitment, as it needs constant maintenance and care. Given this, it will live forever (there are still craft on the water today, in good condition, built in the early 1800s) and should retain its value. If the maintenance schedule is not carried out then the craft will deteriorate, lose value and could, in the worst-case scenario, sink.

It is essential to keep up regular maintenance, as will be discussed later.

SIMILAR CRAFT

The inland waterways are, of course, home to other types of craft than narrow boats. The rivers have all sorts of craft on them, some sea-going and some designed specifically for use on inland waters. The canals have a more restricted list of craft types although the odd unusual vessel can still be found.

Cruisers

Cruisers appeared on the canals as trading craft became less common, either rotting away or becoming the home of the crew who used to work them. They were used by those wishing to take short trips along what was left (at the time) of our canal system.

Early cruisers were made of wood but GRP (glass reinforced plastic) soon took over. Some early pleasure craft were also made from obsolete narrow boats – these were cut in half and a new bow was put on the stern and a new stern on the bow. This gave

There are many different types of GRP (glass reinforced plastic) cruisers on the canal system and this is just one example. Most are powered by outboard petrol engines, although inboard petrol and diesel engines can also be found, as well as electric outboards.

two 40ft (12.2m) boats out of one 71ft 6in (21.8m) one. They, of course, had steel hulls but often had GRP 'lids' and many of them looked identical.

Cruisers are normally powered by a petrol outboard, although a few diesel and electric outboards exist, and some cruisers have inboard engines – either petrol and diesel.

While cruisers are mainly leisure craft, a small number are used for commercial or residential purposes, although the space limitations do cause a problem.

Most cruisers are not as stable as narrow boats or barges because they are lighter. GRP craft can develop a problem with the hull called osmosis, which results from grazing the gel coat on the lock side, for example, which allows water to get into the fibre.

The number of cruisers is in decline today but there are still a fair few around.

Short Boats

Short boats are a type of barge but deserve their own heading because they were built to navigate the northern canals. Built in the same way as narrow boats, they were either 57ft long by 14ft beam (17.4m by 4.3m) or 62ft long by 14ft 4in or 14ft 6in beam (18.9m by 14.35 or 14.4m). A few have found their way south (the normal way is by lorry, although some have made the trip down the east coast).

Such craft were built until the 1950s and there are still a few examples around, mainly in residential use or as passenger craft.

The railways of the UK were originally built to different gauges – 4ft 8.5in, 5ft 3in, 5ft 6in and 7ft 0.25in (1.4m, 1.6m, 1.7m, 2.1m), but over the years these settled down to two and then finally one gauge, 4ft 8.5in (1.4m), to enable traffic to be carried in one wagon across the country between railway companies.

Farnworth *started life as a cargo-carrying craft. It was then converted to a passenger trip boat and is now in use as a residence.*

18 TYPES OF CRAFT

ABOVE: *A Thames barge on the River Medway at Rochester.*

A Dutch-style barge on the Grand Union Canal in use as a residence. The wheelhouse can be lowered to enable the boat to pass under low bridges. Such craft can only navigate on wider waterways.

A modern wide-beam canal cruiser built in the same way as a modern steel narrow boat but to a wider beam (width), which can vary between 10ft and 14ft (3m–4.2m).

The canal network had the same problem but this was never resolved, so today we have the narrow canals of the Midlands, the short canals of the north and the barge canals of the south.

Most short boats, which were used between Wigan and Leeds, are still in the north but a few in the south and have found a life in commercial use in one form or another. Some have been turned into floating homes.

There are fewer short boats about, but then more narrow boats than short boats were built as they could operate on both the Midlands network and the southern waterways.

Barges

In addition to short boats, there are many types of barge found on the inland waterways. Each region of England produced its own style of craft, from Thames barges to trows, flats, wherries, keels and sloops.

In addition, for use on the western end of the Leeds and Liverpool Canal and the Bridgewater, we have a larger version of the short boat called a long boat (not to be confused with the craft used by the Vikings or, indeed, narrow boats, which were called long boats on the River Severn!). The locks in this area were larger and thus allowed passage to longer craft. The main cargo was coal.

Few examples of any these craft exist today, although a number of Thames barges and keels have made it into the twenty-first century. Quite a few are in use on the Thames, mainly as residential craft.

A number of craft have also made it across the Channel from France, Belgium and (mainly) Holland. The most popular Dutch barges (not to be confused with modern craft built in the UK called 'Dutch barges', which are built to similar lines) are Tjalks. These, like other Dutch types such as Aaks, come in different sizes depending on the work they were originally designed for and the waterways they were expected to navigate. Replica boats are also being built today in boatyards, both in the UK and on the continent, specifically for private pleasure and residential use.

If you have an interest in the various types of barge built in Holland, there is an excellent museum (housed on a boat, of course) in Amsterdam.

Some boats being built today are to narrow boat design but wider than 7ft (2.1m) beam. These are known as 'wide beams' and fall into the 'barge' category. I have heard the term 'wide-beam narrow boat', but, logic dictates you cannot have something that is both wide and narrow!

Such craft are, of course, restricted in the routes available as they are unable to use the narrow canals of the Midlands. The bulk of these boats are used on the Grand Union main line, the Thames and the Kennet and Avon, although they do sometimes turn up in other locations as well.

Houseboats

This is a term used to describe (nor-mally unpowered) craft used for residential purposes; they can be craft converted for such use or built specifically as houseboats. The latter are best described as a pontoon with a structure built on top and, indeed, many are simply that – a pontoon with a mobile home sitting on top. Of course, many powered craft are also used residentially but the description given to these is the normal one used for such craft (rather than 'houseboat').

Many houseboats have been pur-pose-built for certain locations, such as marinas and lakes, to provide housing in the same way that mobile homes have replaced prefabs.

Houseboats can be converted from older craft with the engine removed or can be a new construction with a pontoon with a structure placed on top. Underwater maintenance of the hull can present a problem especially if the structure is two storeys – it is difficult to get to dry dock with canal bridges in the way.

TYPES OF CRAFT 21

While some some houseboats will be used for commercial purposes, such as are used as clubhouses or offices, most are built for living on.

The main problem with such craft is often underwater maintenance, as the craft needs to be towed to a dry dock for work to be carried out.

MODERN NARROW BOAT LAYOUTS

The narrow boat today will normally be constructed of mild steel and propelled by a diesel engine. There are many uses for both original narrow boats and modern craft as described above.

Modern narrow boats come with three different layouts at the rear:

Traditional (trad) The cabin comes almost to the back of the boat, providing a small deck space with the steerer standing in the step just inside the back door. This is based on the original design of former working boats. In this design the engine can be situated forward of the back cabin, as on ex-working craft, or right at the stern. In either case, the exhaust is normally trunked to come out of the roof through a thin chimney with a 'cutter'. The cutter is the brass circle at the top of the exhaust pipe which cuts the blast from the exhaust and prevents the steerer from being covered by muck blasted by the exhaust from the roof of a tunnel.

Cruiser stern These craft have a much larger open back deck, providing space for those on the craft to congregate (and get in the way of the steerer!). They are great for short trips but not so practical for long-distance boating.

Semi-trad This design has the same deck space as the cruiser stern but enclosed with cabin walls (but no roof), so sideways on it looks the same as a traditional boat. Here the engine is housed in an engine bay under the back deck at the stern.

The three distinct stern types have different advantages. The traditional stern offers the steerer some

A semi-trad gives the lines of a traditional stern but with the space provided by a cruiser stern for guests on board - a sort of half-way house between the two.

protection in wet or cold conditions but provides little space. The living area being in the back cabin of the boat also gives the steerer easy access to the heat from the back cabin stove and the ability to make a hot drink while still operating the boat. A cruiser stern has a much bigger back deck with the engine underneath. This is a more sociable arrangement, as it allows the friends who are with you on the trip to gather on the back deck, and also provides easier access to the engine for maintenance. A semi-trad provides the look of a

22 | TYPES OF CRAFT

The cutter is a loop of metal on top of the exhaust stack. It is there to avoid the exhaust blast from taking muck off the roof of a tunnel and covering the back cabin and steerer with dirt and brick dust.

traditional stern but with the benefits of a cruiser stern.

My own boat was built with a cruiser stern but within a year I had it converted to a traditional outline, although the back cabin contains the engine. On a true traditional stern, the engine is housed forward of the back cabin and in an unconverted craft often houses the loo.

THE EXTERIOR

This section relates to narrow boats but can also apply to other types of craft.

The tiller, at the back, or stern, of the craft, is connected to the rudder. The propeller pushes water from in front of it and propels the craft through the water. This provides forward thrust (of course, in reverse, the boat will go backwards). The flow of water travels over the rudder and if this is turned one way or the other, this will change the direction of the boat.

The rudder is connected to the tiller, which is often S-shaped and this is what the steerer will move to adjust the boat's direction. To allow easy access to the back cabin of a craft with a traditional stern, the tiller itself is removable. It is kept in place with a tiller pin, which is often a brass ornament but can be a simple screwdriver!

On a narrow boat it is normal to have painted 'counter bands' round the stern. It is thought that this came about to reflect the light from a following craft, making it easier to see. This now forms part of the accepted traditional painting of a narrow boat.

The tiller on a butty boat (or horse-drawn boat) is much larger, as it had to operate a larger rudder – it had to be larger as it did not have the benefit of a propeller forcing water over it. These tillers could be taken out and inverted while the boat was tied up.

At the other end of the boat, at the bow or 'sharp end', there is normally a triangular-shaped upright board called a deck or cratch board. Not found on all modern narrow boats, it served two main purposes on working craft.

The first was as a support for the top plank, which ran down the top of the craft supported by

The tiller of a motor narrow boat is S-shaped and is connected to the rudder at the base. The top has a beam of brass, wood or steel which the steerer uses to rotate the rudder, thus changing the direction of the flow of water from the propeller over the rudder and thus changing the direction of the craft.

The stern of a motor narrow boat, showing the traditional layout at the back of the boat.

24 TYPES OF CRAFT

ABOVE: *The butty of this pair has had the tiller removed as the craft are breasted (tied side by side) and thus the butty does not need steering. The rudder is much larger as it has to push against the flow of water passing the boat rather than having the water being pushed back over it by the propeller of a motor boat.*

A cratch board without a tunnel lamp on it.

Narrow boats are fitted with fenders fore and aft. At the fore end the fender is to stop damage to lock gates and so on, and at the stern to stop the rudder being caught in the mitre of a lock gate. The fender on the stern of a motor boat and at the bow of a butty also prevent damage when the latter is being towed.

two stands and a mast in the hold. The top plank was used to support the tarpaulins (or cloths) that covered the cargo to protect it from the elements and, to some degree, from theft.

Secondly, the cratch board helped to prevent any water coming into the bow – over a lock gate, for example – from flooding into the boat.

A modern use, in addition to protecting the bow from ingress of water from a lock, is to form one end of a tent made using a cratch cover, which also prevents rainwater getting into the bow space. In the tent area you will often find seating and such things below as gas and water lockers.

At both ends of the boat there will be fenders, usually made of rope. The one at the front cushions the impact when the boat surges forward in a lock, protecting both the lock gate and the craft and its contents. The one at the rear, called a button, protects the rudder. Fenders should be fitted with a weak link (*see* Chapter 8).

Most craft are also fitted with side fenders to put down the side of the boat if you are moored to another craft, to prevent the boats from banging into each other or into the bank, and to protect the craft from other craft speeding past. Side fenders are sausage-shaped and made of either rope or rubber. You should not use tyres as side fenders, nor should you have side fenders down when the craft is moving (except on certain waterways, such as the Nene).

At the top of the cratch, or at some other high point at the front of the boat, there will be a tunnel lamp. This is designed to show other boats where you are in a tunnel – not to blind them! It can also be used to provide some light when boating after dark, but it is not a headlight!

Other lights on the outside of a narrow boat might be navigation lights. Not all boats are fitted with these as they are not required on the canal system unless you intend to travel on a river in the dark.

A shaft, or barge pole, is helpful if you get 'stemmed up' (run aground), while a boarding plank helps you get on and off – both of these can be kept on the roof. A shorter pole (called a cabin shaft) is often kept at the stern in reach of the steerer. A cabin shaft will usually have a hook at one end in case you need to fish items out of the canal.

THE INTERIOR

Again, the inside of a narrow boat will be very much like other types of craft, such as a barge. The main difference, of course, is the fact that the beam of the boat, at 6ft 10in (2m), imposes some limitations compared to a wider craft.

On a modern boat, the layout is up to the individual preference of the owner and what they want to

The inside of the Spirit. The layout of modern boats differs from craft to craft. This shot, from halfway down the craft looking forward, shows the living area with the fire. Behind this is the dining room and then the kitchen or galley, leading in turn to the front deck.

One half of a galley showing the cooker. A boat cooker can be supplied as one unit or with the hob separate from the oven.

use the craft for, but will include a galley or kitchen, a living area, one or more bedrooms and a bathroom.

Equipment will be covered in greater detail later in this book (see Chapter 9), but mention should be made here of some of the items that may be found inside a boat today.

You will, of course, need cutlery, crockery and cooking equipment, such as saucepans and so on, as well as other standard kitchen items. You will also need towels and other bathroom items, wet weather clothing, maps and guides, a television and something to play music on. The list of personal effects you might want to keep on board is endless; of course, if the boat is your home you will have all of your household goods, personal effects and valuables on board with you. You should remember to account for such items in your insurance cover and should discuss this with your insurance provider.

Fire extinguishers are required by the Boat Safety Scheme, and how many you need is determined by the size of the boat. Most people use dry powder, but be warned – if used, the clean-up operation afterwards is a nightmare. I prefer CO_2 and have both on my boat. The Boat Safety Scheme, compliance with which is a requirement for all craft licensed on CRT (Canal and River Trust) waterways, also requires that a fire blanket is provided in the galley.

Many narrow boat owners like to follow traditional schemes of internal decoration, and adorn their cabins with plaques and lace plates, items of painted canal ware, brass items and rag rugs.

Plaques are issued to boat owners who attend boat rallies and festivals and many boat owners screw them to the inside of boat doors or other locations. They are normally made of brass.

Lace plates (or ribbon plates) have been a popular decoration for the inside of narrow boat cabins for over 100 years and are much sought after by boat owners. It is possible to obtain modern versions, but it is the originals that are most desirable, and some such plates can be quite valuable. Of course, these items are delicate and can be easily damaged if your boat bumps in a lock or hits a bridge hole, which can happen no matter how careful you are.

Both dry powder and CO_2 extinguishers can be used on boats as long as the correct rating is carried to comply with the Boat Safety Scheme for the size of craft.

Lace or ribbon plates were designed as souvenirs and many say something like 'a present from Brighton'. They became popular with the working boat families to decorate the back cabins of their boats.

TYPES OF CRAFT

Canal ware can be any item painted in the traditional 'roses and castles' fashion, but small Buckby water cans, dippers (a metal bowl with a handle), coal scuttles and small stools are the most popular.

Rag rugs are made by looping bits of rag through a hessian backing to make small rugs for use inside a narrow boat back cabin.

Both canal ware and rag rugs are often sold in museum shops and are made locally by boat owners and others for sale at such locations. Such enterprise helps to keep these traditions alive, and many items now decorate homes as well as boats.

A modern 'tradition' is 'Rosie and Jim' dolls, which come from a television show for children from the 1980s. Many narrow boat owners put a pair of such dolls looking out of a porthole window on their boat.

Various items of canal ware including a small rag rug.

Rosie and Jim were two television puppets from a children's programme. They lived on a narrow boat and the canal network took to them; many boats contain a pair of such dolls – often looking out of the window.

CHAPTER 3

CRAFT USES

Narrow boats, both ex-commercial and modern builds, not to mention other craft, are used on our inland waterways for many different things. This chapter covers the most common modern-day uses of these craft.

There are many new boats being built, but few of these are the traditional 71ft 6in (21.8m) in length. Most are 57ft 6in (17.5m) or 60ft (18.3m), as this is the optimum size to navigate the entire inland waterways system, including the northern network. Narrow boats are today built in sizes from 20ft (6m) to 70ft (21.3m), mainly in steel.

The largest number of craft are used for private pleasure. The next largest group is residential use – and this group is growing. Then there is still a fair proportion of craft used for commercial purposes albeit not for carrying goods.

COMMERCIAL USES

The original use of the canals was, of course, commercial. Narrow boats were built to a standard size to fit the locks of the Midlands canals – 71ft 6in (21.8m) long by 7ft (2.1m) beam (width). Originally the craft were horse-drawn, which caused a problem when it came to getting the craft through tunnels, most of which were built without towpaths. Later narrow boats were built as, or were converted to, motor boats.

Early examples were fitted with steam engines, but the size of the engine and boiler plus the coal to fuel the engine took up too much valuable cargo space, and the new (at the time) invention of 'heavy oil' engines proved to be a much better way of propelling boats. Even loaded with 25 tons of cargo

A pair of working narrow boats working breasted (tied side by side) heading south on the Grand Union Canal. Where the distance between locks was short it was easier to keep the boats tied in this way, but over longer distances it was easier and quicker to tow the butty behind the motor.

there was still spare power available from the engine and so such boats were teamed up with a 'butty' boat. These were originally simply horse boats, but later unpowered butty boats were built specifically to pair up with motor boats.

During the mid-1900s the commercial use of the waterways declined as goods were transported by rail or road. Waterways fell into disuse and the fleets of narrow boats were, in the main, either cut up or converted into pleasure craft. Nonetheless, there is still a wide range of commercial uses for craft today. Many ex-working narrow boats are either still being used in their original state (as maintenance craft or for carrying goods, for example) or have been converted to a new role.

Modern commercial uses of craft include hotel boats, camping boats, trip boats, restaurant boats and bars (both moving and static), nightclubs (again, both moving and static). All of these, if there are more than twelve passengers on board (except for craft permanently moored), need an MCA (Marine and Coastguard Agency) certificate following an inspection to confirm the number of passengers that can be carried safely.

This is not to say that craft used commercially but permanently moored do not need to be inspected. While the MCA only has jurisdiction over craft that move, the relevant navigation authority will usually require a Boat Safety Certificate to be issued following an inspection, and the local authority should also show an interest.

There are many local trip boats run either on a commercial basis or by local canal societies for those wanting a short taste of canal travel. The latter

There are many trip boats providing short trips for the public normally on a pay-as-you-go basis. Most boats of this type, like the one shown here, carry a maximum of twelve passengers. Any more, and the craft has to comply with the regulations of the MCA (Marine and Coastguard Agency), which imposes a number of safety conditions on the owners of the craft that are checked by a surveyor on a regular basis. Carrying twelve or fewer passengers still requires stringent safety checks but these are imposed by the navigation authority instead and the craft are only inspected every four years.

CRAFT USES

A floating café at Little Venice near Paddington, with seating both inside and out. This is the most common type of floating shop but there are many other varieties out on the waterways, both static and moving. They sell everything from cheese to sweets.

often have special events for children, and some work with local schools to provide a learning experience as part of the school curriculum.

Shops

Floating shops, both static and mobile, have been around for years but are becoming a growing phenomenon, offering everything from cups of coffee to books, and cheese to iron work. While some craft are moored in the same spot all the time, others move round the system in a 'floating market'. Often a group will get together and arrange to meet on a weekend at a specific location in a kind of pop-up market, which brings in additional custom.

At some locations, such as Little Venice in London and Stratford Basin in Stratford-upon-Avon, floating shops are permanently moored and thus provide a regular service to locals and tourists.

Pleasure Boat Hire

Hire boats are available for both day trips and weekly hire.

A day hire boat will be used by groups on a self-drive basis, often for a family day out with a picnic either on board or just off the boat at a suitable spot. Such craft are provided with a toilet and simple cooking facilities and have an inside cabin and a seating area in the bow.

Weekly hire craft are for smaller groups who want to take a one- or two-week holiday and these provide sleeping accommodation as well as somewhere to cook. Some firms with more than one base can offer a point-to-point trip rather than an out and back voyage, although most hire firms have only one base. However, in many cases, you can take a circular route to avoid coming back the same way.

Many craft also offer trips for the disabled, both short day trips and longer trips with overnight facilities, while other community craft offer basic camping or, again, day trips.

Commercial Carrying and Maintenance Craft

There are still commercial carrying craft and finally work boats used for canal maintenance.

The bulk of the commercial carrying today is aggregates. Some coal is still carried but most such craft fill up with coal (and often diesel and sometimes LPG cylinders) and sell to boat owners and canalside properties on their way round the system, returning to refill once the bulk of the cargo has been sold. Perhaps these should really be counted as floating shops.

Maintenance craft are many and varied, from specific dredging craft and hoppers to maintenance 'flats' used as mobile workshops around the system.

A commercial craft requires a commercial licence from the relevant navigation authority and the cost of insurance will be higher. The Boat Safety Scheme inspection also has more requirements for some commercial uses.

PRIVATE PLEASURE USE

The bulk of craft on the inland waterways today are used by their owners for cruising around the country. Most are based at a home mooring, though some are used round the system. There are a number of ex-working craft in such use both in their original condition or converted with a superstructure added. The majority, however, are modern craft built of welded steel with, in the main, diesel engines. The length of such craft can be anything from 23ft (7m) to 70ft (21.3m) but the beam, or width, of 6ft 10in (2m) is always standard.

Over the last fifty years or so, the boatyards around the system have increased the number of craft on the network at a steady rate. A yard will either start from scratch, building the hull and then lining and fitting out the inside, or will order a hull and superstructure from a steel fabricator and then line and fit out to the requirement of the prospective new owner. Most craft are built to order, although a small number are built as stock boats.

Most of these boats are owned by one owner (or family) but sometimes two couples or a group will jointly own a boat and share the use of it – and, of course, the running costs.

Some companies actually run 'shared ownership' craft, although here you have no say in who your joint owners are. A big advantage of this scheme is that all maintenance and administration, such as BSS inspections, licence and insurance, is dealt with on your behalf (*see* Chapter 5).

RESIDENTIAL USE

There have always been residential craft in use on the waterway system. Indeed, for the first fourteen

A modern steel narrow boat. Most of modern craft are built to a shorter length than the old standard length of 71ft 6in (21.8m).

CRAFT USES

A ship's lifeboat converted to a houseboat. A narrow boat or barge looks the same whether used for leisure or living on.

years of owning my own boat, *Spirit*, we lived on board.

In the days of canal carrying, the crew – often a husband and wife team (sometimes with children on board) – lived on the boat in the rather small back cabin (in the case of a pair of boats, two back cabins). In the last century such people lived on boats mainly because they were canal enthusiasts.

In the 2000s, however, the number of residential craft has increased dramatically, especially in city centres, due to the high cost of housing. Boats that do not have a registered mooring have to move every fourteen days, which can cause problems for the Canal and River Trust. The Constant Cruising Licence was designed for boats travelling round the entire system, while most of these modern 'liveaboards' tend to stay within about 30 miles (50km) or so of the same spot, and as such locations tend to be city or town centres, issues with congestion start to increase in such areas.

The problem is, of course, that a shortage of linear moorings puts cruising boats in such areas at a disadvantage as they find nowhere to moor.

Buy to Let

A recent popular trend has been buying a boat to re-let it for residential use. The problem with this is that such use infringes the terms of a private pleasure craft licence and this creates a problem. The navigation authority may allow the boat owner to purchase a commercial licence for the craft at a much higher fee. You also need a commercial Boat Safety Scheme certificate, which requires compliance with a greater number of items.

The other problem is insurance. Again, use of the craft in this way could invalidate the policy if it is insured for private pleasure use – indeed any use of the craft for financial gain will cause a problem. You need to check with a potential Insurer that they are happy for the intended use, which could result in a higher premium.

CHAPTER 4

THE INLAND WATERWAYS

The inland waterways system is made up of three types of waterway, which are, in the main, interconnected – rivers, navigations and canals (*see below*).

The development of the network was prompted by the need to transport goods from one part of the country to another and this was the reason that canals were built – specifically to meet the need to move goods.

The system we have today pre-dates the road and rail networks for the transport of goods. Thanks to the efforts of the Inland Waterways Association and other bodies, we have a good percentage of it left, and much that has been lost is being reclaimed.

The Inland Waterways Association is the longest standing and largest organization set up by volunteers to campaign actively for the retention of our waterways system. Formed in 1946, it holds regular meetings at its many local branches throughout the country and also organizes fund-raising events such as rallies. It also has a working party organization, the Waterway Recovery Group, where members can join in work camps to help restore derelict waterways around the system.

While early waterways were built by the Romans, most of our constructed waterways were built in the late 1700s and 1800s to provide the neces-

The River Thames at Reading. Rivers start off very small then joining with others and become wider as they get closer to the coast until they reach the sea.

sary transport infrastructure for the Industrial Revolution.

At a time when the main way to move goods around the country was by horse and cart on poorly maintained roads and tracks, the canal network offered a huge benefit. Goods could be moved at a much quicker speed and with less risk of breakage in transit than on a cart, and, of course, a narrow boat could carry a much greater tonnage for the same amount of horsepower.

TYPES OF WATERWAY

Inland waterways can be split into three main types:

Rivers, which are natural. In order to be navigable, rivers need to have locks built on them to maintain the levels for navigation throughout the length of the waterway. A natural river has shallows and most meander their way to the sea – both of which cause problems to a loaded boat trying to navigate them.

Navigations are rivers which have been re-routed. Rivers naturally take the easiest route from source to sea, and thus bends and loops form. A navigation is built to cut out such deviations and thus shorten the route. A good example is a 'lock cut', which will enable a craft to leave the river and work through a lock to return to the river at a lower point. The main river takes a longer route and goes over a weir or through shallows on the way.

Canals are totally man-made waterways that were cut (hence the use of the word 'cut' as an alternative to canal) where no river flowed. Such waterways were built by vast teams of men, known as navigators (or navvies), who went on in later years to build the nation's railways. A canal would have been

This shot through the bridge hole at the bottom of a narrow lock says it all!

A typical canalside warehouse.

Top lock on the Marsworth flight on the Grand Union Canal with the second lock in the background. A normal 'flight' has a pound in between locks to enable craft to pass each other.

created for a specific cargo, such as coal, to be transported from pit head to dock (as an example) but along the way boats would call at local wharves, which would increase the traffic on the waterway and the income of the company.

Engineers had to design the route to enable craft to get from A to B and, of course, they had to get round, over or under any hills that stood in the way. Water supply had to be maintained, and so water was stored to supply the system, while locks and tunnels provided the way over or under hills. It was thus not just a case of digging a long ditch. Such items as sources of additional income from goods, water supply and topography all had to be taken into account when planning the route.

All along these waterways, which were originally constructed for the transport of goods, you will find commercial properties built for the service of the transport system, such as boat repair yards and warehouses.

HISTORY OF THE CANAL SYSTEM

The use of inland waterways for transport goes back to Roman times, but canals and navigations were few and far between. The problem was getting such waterways to change level – an essential requirement given the topography of the land.

It was not until the Duke of Bridgewater commissioned engineer James Brindley to construct an artificial waterway from Worsley in an Act of Parliament passed in 1759 that canal building really got under way. The Bridgewater Canal opened in 1761 and included an aqueduct over the River Irwell.

Following the success of this venture there was an explosion of canals being built throughout the land to transport goods – raw materials to the factories and then the finished goods away.

Until this time goods had to be transported, in the main, by cart or packhorse, which was much slower.

In order to keep the water level, the early canals followed the contour of the land, which made the

A staircase flight is where one lock leads straight into the next. On narrow canals, craft are not able to pass in a staircase flight.

canal less expensive to build but increased the time it took to work a boat from one place to another. Later canals took a more direct route, necessitating a more expensive track to build (due to the extensive earthworks required) but resulting in a quicker journey time. This was important, as other, rival forms of transport were now becoming available.

Water levels were changed by locks. These were just over 7ft (2.1m) wide in the Midlands canals but in later years the locks on some canals were either built to twice this width (wide locks) or converted to this size to enable a motor boat and butty to work through as a pair. You can still find evidence of old single locks alongside the wide locks on the Grand Union from Leighton Buzzard to Marsworth. The locks on this stretch were doubled, leaving the old single lock in place, but over time these single locks fell into disuse and were filled in. There are other examples along the route of the Grand Union.

The canals of the central Midlands, however, were built with locks to take craft of a 7ft (2.1m) beam and remain to this gauge to this day.

Depending on the slope of the land, locks can be found either as a single lock or, where the need to raise or lower the level is more acute, in flights. There are examples of 'staircase' flights, where one lock leads directly into another. Here you have to be sure that there is not a boat already in the staircase before you enter as you are not able to pass midway.

There are other ways to overcome hills. Tunnels abound on the waterway system (as they do on the later railway system) and there were inclined planes, boat lifts and other ingenious devices.

Finally, in order to keep the waterway level when crossing a valley, there are many examples of aqueducts of varying lengths all over the system.

This system of waterways lowered the cost of transport and enabled the Industrial Revolution to take off. Canals were built all over the country, greatly increasing the availability of easily transported raw materials and finished goods.

As time passed, paved roads replaced the cart tracks and railways were invented. Roads were then improved. All three of these developments took traffic away from the inland waterways, although in some places interchange basins kept some local traffic on the water and, indeed, increased it.

Despite the massive increase in boats in the 1930s and an attempted revival in the 1940s and 1950s, the use of waterways as a transportation system for goods was coming to an end (with the exception of a very few cargos).

Boats were sunk or broken up, locks and whole waterways fell into disuse and the end of the system was in sight. Many boats were cut in two and, with a new bow patched onto the stern section and a new stern on the bow section, saw continued life as holiday boats. To start with, most of these were in hire fleets, but over time many passed into private ownership.

THE RESTORATION MOVEMENT

In 1945 a group of canal enthusiasts met to discuss the difficult future the inland waterways network was facing, and in 1946 the Inland Waterways Association was formed. As a result of the campaigning the IWA undertook, we now have much of the system restored and back in use for pleasure craft.

The IWA has around 20,000 members and there is a local branch in every part of the country. These branches organize talks and other events on a monthly basis.

Also part of the IWA is the Waterway Recovery Group, which arranges for its volunteers to rebuild and maintain waterways in their spare time.

Boaters and waterways enthusiasts alike owe a great deal of thanks to those who give their time to campaign for the retention and restoration of our system and to those in the WRG who go out and restore lost waterways, bringing additional mileage back into use.

It is fair to say that without the work of the Inland Waterways Association, many of our waterways would have been lost forever and we would not today have the miles of waterway that currently make up our system. We have still lost many miles of canal but the fight to reinstate many of these is ongoing.

THE INLAND WATERWAYS 39

An interchange basin enabled goods to be transferred between different modes of transport. In this instance there were two sidings above the right-hand side of the basin where goods could be loaded from narrow boats to railway vehicles and vice versa.

For many years the Inland Waterways Association organized an annual festival always on a different part of the network, bringing together up to 900 boats with trade and craft stands. Attended by thousands of visitors, it was designed as a showcase for the inland waterways for about fifty years.

In addition to the IWA, there are many local restoration groups that work with the IWA to keep up or rebuild stretches of waterway, or indeed whole canals; many started with the assistance and support of the association.

The IWA is the largest and longest-standing society but there are others bodies you might consider joining. The National Association of Boat Owners, the Historic Narrow Boat Club and the Residential Boat Owners' Association are the three main national bodies but there are many others for different types of craft, waterways and usage.

There are also many boat clubs dotted around the inland waterways system that provide their members with moorings, often as well as a clubhouse and other facilities. Most such clubs belong in turn to the Association of Waterway Cruising Clubs and thus provide each other's members with moorings while cruising.

NAVIGATION AUTHORITIES

In order to use a boat on the system you need a licence, but there are twenty-nine different navigation authorities within the UK. The IWA has long campaigned for a single National Navigation Authority and this is finally looking more likely but not, sadly, in the short term.

Most navigation authorities (eighteen) belong to the Association of Inland Navigation Authorities

(AINA); between them, these NAs are responsible for somewhere in the region of 5,000 miles (8,000km) of navigable inland waterway in the UK.

The largest authority is the Canal and River Trust (CRT), which took over from the British Waterways Board in England in 2012. They administer just over 2,000 miles (3,200km) of navigable waterways. CRT has a head office in Milton Keynes and is responsible for maintaining the canal system, which is 200 years old on average, so you can imagine the problems that they have with maintenance. BWB still administers the inland waterways in Scotland.

The next largest is the Environment Agency (EA), who look after about 600 miles (1,000km) of navigable rivers and navigations, including the Thames and waterways in the south of England and East Anglia. It is planned that the CRT will take over the navigational functions of the EA; at the time of writing, the two organizations are discussing how this will work. For some rivers administered by the EA, such as the Lea and Severn, the CRT already look after all navigational matters.

The next down in size is the Broads Authority, and all the remaining ones cover one small stretch of waterway. It is likely that many of these will be absorbed by the CRT in the coming years.

CHAPTER 5

BUYING A NARROW BOAT

So, you want to own a narrow boat? The first thing you need to do is to consider whether you can afford it – not just the purchase price, but the ongoing cost of ownership. You also need to decide what you want to own it for – private pleasure, to live on or to operate a business from.

Should you buy new or second-hand? If you decide on a new boat, you have to search for a boat builder who will provide the boat you want, fully fitted, part fitted or simply hull, superstructure and engine. If you opt for second-hand, you have various options available. Boats are advertised online, through dedicated websites and social media pages such as Facebook. You can also tour local marinas and boatyards to see many boats for sale. Finally, of course, there are small ads in the boating press placed directly by the owners.

While most craft sold by a boat builder come ready painted, some are provided in red oxide for the owner to paint, and perhaps fit out, themselves.

BUYING A NARROW BOAT

In all cases, commission a survey before finalizing the purchase and make sure that if you pull out because of something in the survey, you can get your deposit back.

In the case of a commercial project, you need to make sure that the relevant navigation authority will permit your venture and find out exactly what you need to do before the business can operate.

For example, any craft used to carry more than twelve passengers needs to be inspected by a surveyor working on behalf on the Marine and Coastguard Agency to establish the condition of the craft for such use and the maximum number of passengers the craft can carry.

NEW BUILD

Buying a new boat from a boat builder is the most expensive way of getting afloat, but you will have the layout you want and there are other advantages of having a new boat, such as deciding on the name of the craft and the external colour scheme, and the knowledge that the craft hopefully has no defects. Initially, there should also be less maintenance required.

Using a boat builder who is a member of British Marine will give you the protection of knowing that the craft has been built to Recreational Craft Directive standards by competent staff. A list of narrow boat builders who are members of British Marine can be found on the BM website.

It is still a good idea to contact other customers who have used the company to see if they are happy with the service they received.

The cost will differ from yard to yard and, of course, the length of the boat and the standard of fit-out will also affect the price.

Before you decide on your boat layout, it is a good idea to look at other boats of similar length to the one you are considering having built to see what they have done. Some boats have the main entrance at the front, others at the stern. The rest of the layout will be affected by how the main entrance is gained to the craft.

Self Fit-Out

One way of acquiring a new boat while keeping the cost down is to have the boat builder supply you with a hull and engine and then fit the boat out yourself. You must then employ a Gas Safe-registered engineer to install any gas equipment and piping, as you are no longer allowed to install gas yourself. At the end of the fit-out you should ask a surveyor to issue you with documents to confirm that it has been built to conform to the RCD (Recreational Craft Directive) and issue you with a Boat Safety Scheme Certificate.

If you are fitting out your own boat, it is a good idea to plan the layout to allow access to the inside of the hull. It doesn't happen often, but there will be

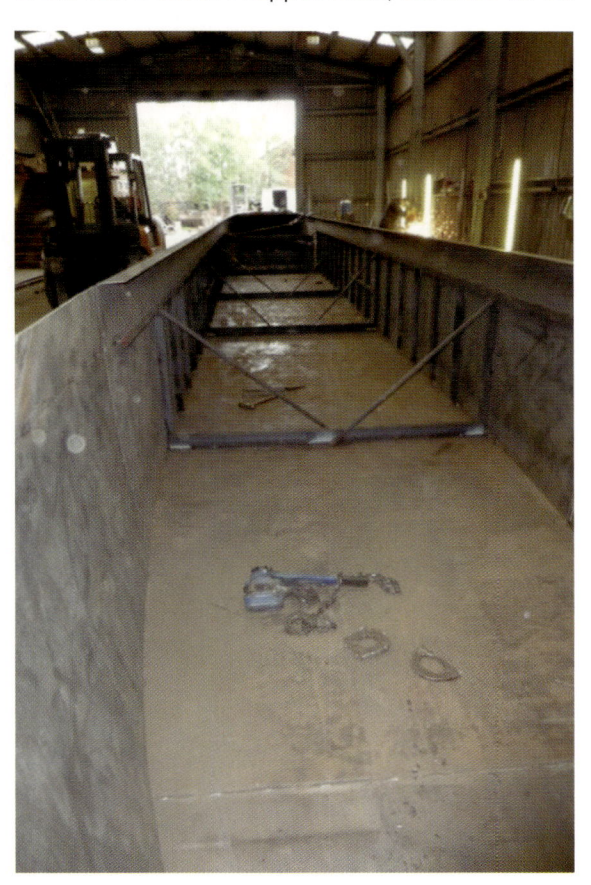

A hull in a workshop waiting for the superstructure to be fitted.

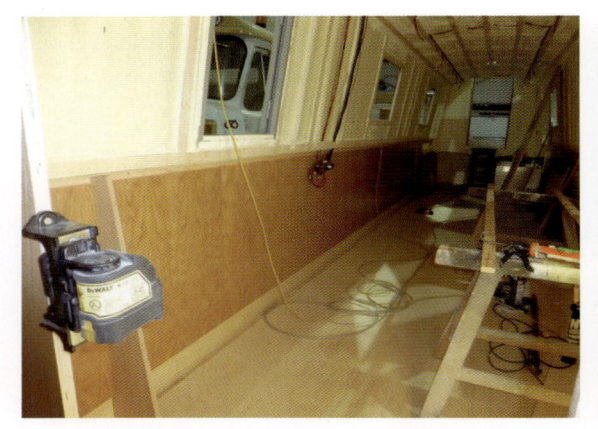

Once the superstructure has been welded on, the engine can be installed and the fitting-out of the craft can begin.

Some craft are supplied to the new owner with hull, superstructure and engine, leaving the inside to be fitted out by another company or by the owner themselves. Once the craft is fitted out, it has to be inspected to confirm that it complies with both RCD and BSS requirements.

times that you need to get at the hull, and you don't want then to have to demolish bulkheads and furniture and rebuild everything afterwards.

I have owned my boat since I had her built in 1975 and, in the 90s, I had the side panels below the gunwale and the floor boards up to wire-brush and paint the inside of the hull. On another occasion I moved a sink outlet and wanted to have the old one blanked off. The boatyard were very impressed that undoing just six screws took them to the correct spot.

You should also remember to build in some inspection hatches in the floor so that you can get in to check the bilges.

Assuming you are starting with a bare hull, you first need to decide where everything is going to go. As with instructing a boatyard to build you a boat, it is a good idea to visit lots of boats to get ideas and then draw out a plan of the boat so that you know what is going to fit where.

First thing to do is to put two or three coats of red oxide on top of the paint the builders have put on. You then need to put in the ballast you will require. There are lots of options here but keep away from loose material such as gravel and do not pour concrete into the bottom of the boat – make sure any ballast is easily removable. I find short lengths of old railway line best (a coat of red oxide on these is a good idea as well) but have it cut into short lengths that are easily moveable if required.

You now need to think about the bulkheads, which are the internal walls of the craft separating the different rooms. Some craft have the floors fitted first and then have the bulkheads fitted to the floor, but you then run into the problem that if you need to get under the floorboards for any reason, the bulkhead has to come down!

The next step is to lay the floor. Marine ply is the answer here and it can be laid on wooden bearers set across the bilges at 2ft (60cm) intervals.

BUYING A NARROW BOAT 45

This is the fire on Spirit. *Note the protection on the wall that prevents the woodwork from overheating and setting fire to the craft. Coal or wood fires on boats are fitted with doors to prevent burning coal and wood falling out with the same result.*

Remember you may need to get these up at some stage in the life of the boat so do not fix them down so that they cannot be removed. Remember also to fit some inspection hatches so that you can look and see what is down there from time to time.

Once the floor is down you can start cladding the sides. Again, bear in mind that you may need to have easy access to the sides of the boat – at least on and below the water line – so build this into your design.

My woodwork teacher always used to say 'measure three times and cut once'.

What heating will you have? Most people go for a solid fuel stove but another popular option is a diesel stove. LPG (gas) heating is a big no, as it puts too much water into the atmosphere (though other LPG appliances such as cookers are fine).

You can run radiators round the boat from a back boiler on a solid fuel stove and this is quite a good combination system as it heats the whole boat, not just the room where the fire is situated.

Where is the fire going? You will, of course, need to have a chimney fitted and protect the woodwork surrounding the fire against overheating with a suitable material. Wood is not a good idea close to a fire. You should not have a flue or fire too close to any woodwork as overheating can cause a fire. (I have dealt with three claims over the years where this has happened resulting in the total loss of the craft.) When putting up the cladding, remember that you will be running wires down the boat and you should install a channel for this. This will normally be under the gunwales but you will also need some wires going into the ceiling for lights.

Keep the gas equipment, such as the cooker, as close as you can to the gas locker. Gas piping has to be either on display or in a channel with an easily removable cover so that it can be readily inspected. Remember that for LPG work, this has to be carried out by a Gas Safe Engineer and you cannot fit this yourself.

Once you have the cladding and bulkheads up you can put in wiring, sockets, switches and other items that will involve the whole length of the boat before starting to install furniture.

Most craft have fitted furniture such as wardrobes and so on, but if you want either to change things round or get at the inside of the hull, this will require dismantling. It is much better to obtain free-standing furniture and connect it to the inside of the boat with angle brackets so it doesn't topple over if the craft should get 'hung up'. You have to do this with the cooker so why not the rest? Of course, there are some things that will have to be built in, such as the cooker, fridge and other white goods, but keep these to a minimum.

Curtains should be fitted in such a way that, if a window is open, the curtain cannot foul a source of flame and catch fire. A bar or rope across the window to hold the curtains in place is one option. Blinds are also popular but, again, these need to be secured.

You should advise your Insurers of the fact that you are fitting the boat out, as the sum to be insured will rise during the fit-out period. If your insurance provider understands the idea of fitting a boat out (remember, most boats are GRP production craft that would not need such attention) they will provide a policy with a maximum value but stating that claims would be based on proof of value at the time of loss. They may seek a valuation of the craft at the end of the fit-out period.

At all times you should refer to the requirements of the Boat Safety Scheme. As an example, many items such as fires and cookers need to be fixed to the craft and should not be free-standing. This is to prevent problems if the craft tips, resulting in any loose equipment falling over.

BUYING SECOND-HAND

There are essentially two main ways of buying a second-hand boat.

The first is direct from the owner, found through word of mouth or an advert. Such adverts appear in the waterways press, which encompasses both paid-for magazines sold in boatyards and main newsagents and free monthly newspapers distributed through boatyards, canal/riverside pubs and club premises.

The second approach is to buy the boat through a boatyard or broker. In the latter case, make sure that the broker is a member of British Marine or the Yacht Brokers, Designers and Surveyors Association (YBDSA). Bear in mind that that the boatyard or broker will usually be acting on behalf of the seller.

Regardless of what you are told, *always* pay for a survey of the craft before you agree to complete the purchase. Even the existing owner may not know of a problem developing with the craft. Assuming the surveyor is a member of one of the main surveying bodies (the most popular one on the inland waterways system is the Yacht Brokers, Designers and Surveyors Association), you will get a factual report on the exact present condition of the craft, backed by their professional indemnity policy. Such a report may contain negative information that may lead you to withdraw your offer, agree a reduced purchase price or arrange for remedial work to be undertaken prior to your purchase of the craft.

If you put a deposit on a boat, make sure that the payment is 'subject to survey', which means that it will be returned in the event of the surveyor finding a major problem with the craft.

Do not forget to take into account such future costs as having a new bottom or new footings (the hull from the chine to the bottom guard) welded on. Your surveyor should undertake an ultrasound survey, which will indicate the original thickness of the hull and the present thickness as well as taking into account pitting, which can occur both on the inside of the hull and the outside.

Always remember that you buy a boat 'as seen', so there is no point in going back to the previous owner with a complaint – they have no legal responsibility to help.

A copy of a Boat Safety Scheme Certificate is helpful but you should bear in mind that this is not a survey – and indeed it says this on the certificate.

Many people buy a second-hand boat and then arrange for a boatyard to refit the interior. Again, once this has happened, your insurance provider may well seek a valuation so they can assess the value to be put onto the policy. Some boat owners do not fully understand how this works. Let us take the example of a boat purchased second-hand for, say, £40,000. It is then taken to a boatyard, who charge a further £40,000 for taking out the parts not wanted and reinstalling the replacement interior. The total cost of the boat to the owner is thus £80,000 but that does not mean the boat is now worth £80,000.

The boatyard will have charged for removing the unwanted bits, which in turn would have had some value.

A marine insurance policy should have a total sum insured for the craft, which represents the sum that the craft, in its present condition, would sell for in a willing-seller, willing-buyer situation.

The problem with narrow boats is that, despite the more or less standard size, they are all individual. Despite the fact that the beam of a narrow boat makes the inside a bit like a corridor, the layout will still differ from one boat to the next. Even the opinion of a marine surveyor who specializes in inland craft is an educated guess, although it at least provides an insurer with a qualified guideline to base the policy on.

All in all, it is a good idea to try boating either by hiring a boat or using a friend's before buying your own.

SHARED OWNERSHIP

One way to reduce the cost of owning a narrow boat or any other craft is to buy it jointly with others. You can either do this yourself with friends or you can buy a part share in a boat.

In the first instance, it is a good idea to have a shared ownership agreement drawn up – just in case!

In the second instance, this is normally arranged through a share ownership company, although there are other ways. Here the number of owners is quite large and you get so many weeks on board for the shares you have. The normal procedure is to buy a share in the craft at the outset (which you can then sell on at a later date) and pay a percentage of the running costs during each year of ownership.

This has the advantage of the company looking after maintenance, craft licence, insurance and mooring. The disadvantage is you may have little choice in where you collect and leave the boat at the start and end of your trip and, of course, you will only have access to the craft during your allotted weeks. Nonetheless, this is a low-cost way to get afloat and many shared ownership boaters have gone on to buy a boat of their own once bitten by the bug.

In any of these situations you have to accept that, at the start of your week, the boat will be where the last owner left it and therefore you will not have any choice of the waterway that you travel on. Some shared ownership boats are taken from and returned to a marina.

CHAPTER 6

RUNNING COSTS

In addition to the cost of buying the boat in the first place, you will have ongoing costs and these should be taken into account prior to purchase.

In this chapter I will not give any actual prices, as the variation in size and age of the craft – and, of course, time – would make such information meaningless.

LICENCE

In order to keep a craft on a waterway you are required to have a licence from the relevant navigation authority. The cost of this will vary from one navigation authority to another and with the size of the craft, but you can buy a Gold Licence which will provide access to both CRT- and EA-controlled waters. Gold Licences start on 1 January each year.

The cost of such a licence goes up every year. You need to contact the navigation authority concerned to discover the cost for the boat you are intending to buy. In most cases, prior to obtaining a licence, you will have to provide evidence that you have at least third-party insurance (usually simply a declaration including the name of the insurer and your policy number) and the number from your craft inspection document showing that you comply with the compulsory parts of the Boat Safety Scheme relevant to the use of the craft.

The licence should be displayed on the craft where navigation authority staff can inspect it.

In the majority of cases you will also have a craft registration number, which will need to be painted on each side of the boat, or you will be provided with number plates. New craft or craft not registered with that authority before will be issued with a new number, while existing craft will normally (but not always) keep the same number.

At the time of writing, discussions are taking place that could result in the CRT taking on the navigational duties of the EA.

MOORINGS

In most cases you will need to have a mooring for the craft.

On the CRT system you can apply for a Constant Cruising Licence, but if you are using the craft in the same area you need to keep it somewhere while it's not in use. A Constant Cruiser has to move the boat every fourteen days to ensure that moorings are available to all craft on the move. This licence is designed for boat owners who cruise the system for all or part of the year.

There are two types of mooring: privately owned, such as those provided by marinas in a basin or on line; and linear (that is, along the bank) on the offside of the waterway and those provided by the navigation authority along the towpath. This will be the biggest ongoing cost and needs to be in your budget.

Marinas can supply a number of facilities that will not be found on the towpath, but will correspondingly cost more.

Keeping your boat at a boatyard, despite the additional cost, does have advantages. You will have yard staff on hand to undertake any work needed, such as engine servicing and running repairs. There will also be a power supply to charge up batteries and operate power tools, as well as water supply, rubbish and Elsan disposal and other benefits, which may differ from one location to another, such as a clubhouse, showers and so on.

INSURANCE

Marine insurance is a specialist area, so simply going to your local broker may not be a good idea – you need to contact a specialist provider. British Marine can supply a list of insurance members, although not all of them understand canals and/or narrow boats or the needs of their owners, so make sure that the company you are speaking to do not think a butty is a sandwich!

A marine insurance policy will be required to provide a minimum of third-party insurance. This will provide cover for claims made against you by a third party who has suffered a loss as a result of your ownership of the craft and for which they hold you responsible. At the time of writing, most policies provide £3,000,000 indemnity. Such a policy is laid out under the Marine Insurance Act of 1906 unless superseded by the Insurance Act of 2015.

In addition to this, however, you can insure for loss or damage to your own craft caused by sudden or violent means. Here your insurers will meet a claim for the repair or loss of the whole craft or part of it, including, if included in your cover, 'personal effects on board'. This last section is not designed to cover items brought from home but items kept on board the craft but which are not a fixture, such as pots and pans, TVs, lace plates and so on. It will not cover consumable stores.

Your policy will provide cover either on a 'value at time of loss' basis or an agreed value policy – make sure you know which type of policy you are being offered.

The 'personal effects on board' cover is not much help to residential boat owners and some marine insurance companies can issue a separate section to provide cover for all the owner's household goods, personal effects and valuables on a replacement-as-new basis, thus providing the residential boat owner with the same cover as someone who lives in a house. Personal liability will often be included in such cover.

A residential policy may also include cover for items taken off the boat, such as jewellery and photographic equipment, and also bicycles.

Other bolt-ons to a marine policy can include such things as personal accident cover, marine legal protection cover, no claims bonus protection and river and canal rescue (check if you have to pay a call-out charge for this).

Do not assume something is covered – ask! It is often the case that something could have been covered, but as the boat owner did not mention it at the time of proposal (or at time of purchase if this is later), it was not. It is a good idea to have a list of questions in front of you when you ring for a quote these days, now that most insurance providers no longer require proposal forms. This is the same with any type of insurance contract.

A classic example here is a portable generator, if you have one. Some companies will not pay for theft of a generator if they do not have it recorded that you have one. The serial number, age and value will be questions that should be requested.

The cost of insurance will depend on the value of the craft and other factors, including any additional covers selected.

MAINTENANCE

This is not a fixed cost – you may spend nothing in one year and thousands in another. Ongoing maintenance is essential, however, and regular contact with your surveyor is recommended. A professional eye can spot a potential problem that the boat owner may not notice.

The protection of the hull (*see* Chapter 7) with a regular application of either black varnish (a bitumen-based product), or a two-coat epoxy is vital for the future of the craft, so you will need to budget for a dry docking. You can then black the hull and arrange for a surveyor to undertake a hull survey at the same time.

A two-coat epoxy will cost more but will give a much longer-lasting protective coat to the steel. This should be applied to a hull just after it has been grit- or sand-blasted. Do not mix epoxy with varnish!

Of course, if you are good at DIY, you can undertake much of such maintenance work yourself. If not, you will need to increase the amount of money you reserve for such work.

It is vital to check all oil levels in your engine on a regular basis, both engine and gearbox, and to keep the stern tube greased; this will prevent water from getting into the hull and also prevent wear on the prop shaft and stern tube. This is dealt with in more detail in Chapter 11.

Whenever you dock the boat, you should check, or have checked for you, the propeller, both for damage to the blades and the connection to the shaft, making sure that the split pin is in good order.

Also check to make sure that the skeg has not been damaged. This is the metal bar that runs from the back of the swim under the propeller to a point under the rudder. The rudder sits in a cup at the end of the skeg, which allows the rudder to turn and keeps it in place. It can become damaged by contact with, for example, the cill in a lock.

You should also check that the sacrificial chine is not worn. This is the part of the boat where the side of the boat meets the bottom, and the bottom usually sticks out about half an inch to protect the weld holding the two parts to each other. Over the years this can become worn by such things as rubbing against lock sides and so on.

Checking on the life left in your sacrificial anodes (metal sections welded to the underside of the hull that protect it against corrosion) is also a must if your boat is out of the water – anodes are best replaced when they are two-thirds used.

Of course, if you are having a surveyor check the craft, the inspection will include checking such points and the written report will state any work that needs undertaking or will need to be undertaken prior to or at the next docking.

OVERWINTERING

If you are not using your boat over the winter period, it is important to take some precautions before leaving the craft. You should ensure that there is adequate anti-freeze in any circulatory systems,

Most modern narrow boats have a gas water-heater fitted. These have to be professionally fitted with exhaust gases venting over the side.

such as central heating, from the back of the stove, or a keel cooling system.

You should also either drain your fresh water system or introduce pink antifreeze, available from most chandlers, which is not harmful if drunk (although I still would not advise it!). It is important to make sure that the entire water system is protected so that you do not run the risk of freezing at any point in your plumbing. The most important part to treat is the water heater – this is likely to be the first part of your boat to freeze and could result, in the worst situation, in the need to fit a replacement.

When reversing the system in the spring, fill your tank and run it through to clear out the pink antifreeze and then run it through again to make sure you have clean water in your system.

The alternative is to empty out the entire system, which can take some time. If you go for this option you again need to make sure that your water heater is protected by blowing down the pipe.

If you use your boat during the winter months, and many do, you will need to consider what action you need to take to prevent damage. Some boat owners drain the water system in between each trip.

Residential craft are, of course, lived on during the winter months but the fire will keep the inside of the boat warm and thus, unless the craft is to be left unoccupied for more than a few days, the problem of freezing pipes can often be discounted (but do consider any piping that is outside the cabin area).

BOAT SAFETY SCHEME AND SURVEYS

The Boat Safety Scheme certificate is a required inspection that was first launched by the British Waterways Board in 1978 as the Certificate of Compliance. This was not compulsory. In 1991 it was changed to the Boat Safety Scheme, and this became compulsory in 1998. The Certificate of Compliance included a hull inspection, but this was excluded from the BSS.

A BSS certificate is valid for four years, but you should remember that if you undertake any alterations to the boat that affect the equipment fitted this will invalidate the certificate and a new one will have to be obtained.

There are two different certificates – one for private craft, with compulsory and advisory checks, and one for commercial craft, for which the advisory items are compulsory.

It should be stressed again that this is not a survey but simply a safety inspection of the equipment on board the craft.

A surveyor or BSS examiner will come to your boat and carry out an inspection and will either decline to issue a certificate, if a serious problem is encountered, or issue a certificate giving a full bill of health or one with advisory comments. In the latter case, you can still renew your craft licence but should take action to resolve the reported problem as soon as possible.

If you are buying a boat you should have a surveyor undertake a survey prior to purchase. This should be a full survey which will tell you everything about the craft – good or bad!

You should have an out-of-the-water survey undertaken every six years by a surveyor, and once the craft reaches a certain age, your Insurer will seek a copy of this prior to renewal of the policy. On the inland waterways system this is twenty-five or thirty years.

A survey is valid for seven years from the date of inspection but most insurance companies will seek a further survey at or before renewal of your policy every six years.

You may ask why – after all, it costs money. As mentioned above, the craft owner cannot be expected to spot a problem that develops over a long time and there are some issues that cannot be picked up without the specialist knowledge and equipment a surveyor will bring with them. In any case, your insurer will require sight of a survey once a boat reaches a certain age – normally after twenty-five years, but this can vary.

Cabin staining can be caused by a number of factors: the two main reasons are muck falling off trees and tar from the boat's chimney. Here you see the latter. Frequent cleaning can resolve both problems.

RUNNING COSTS 53

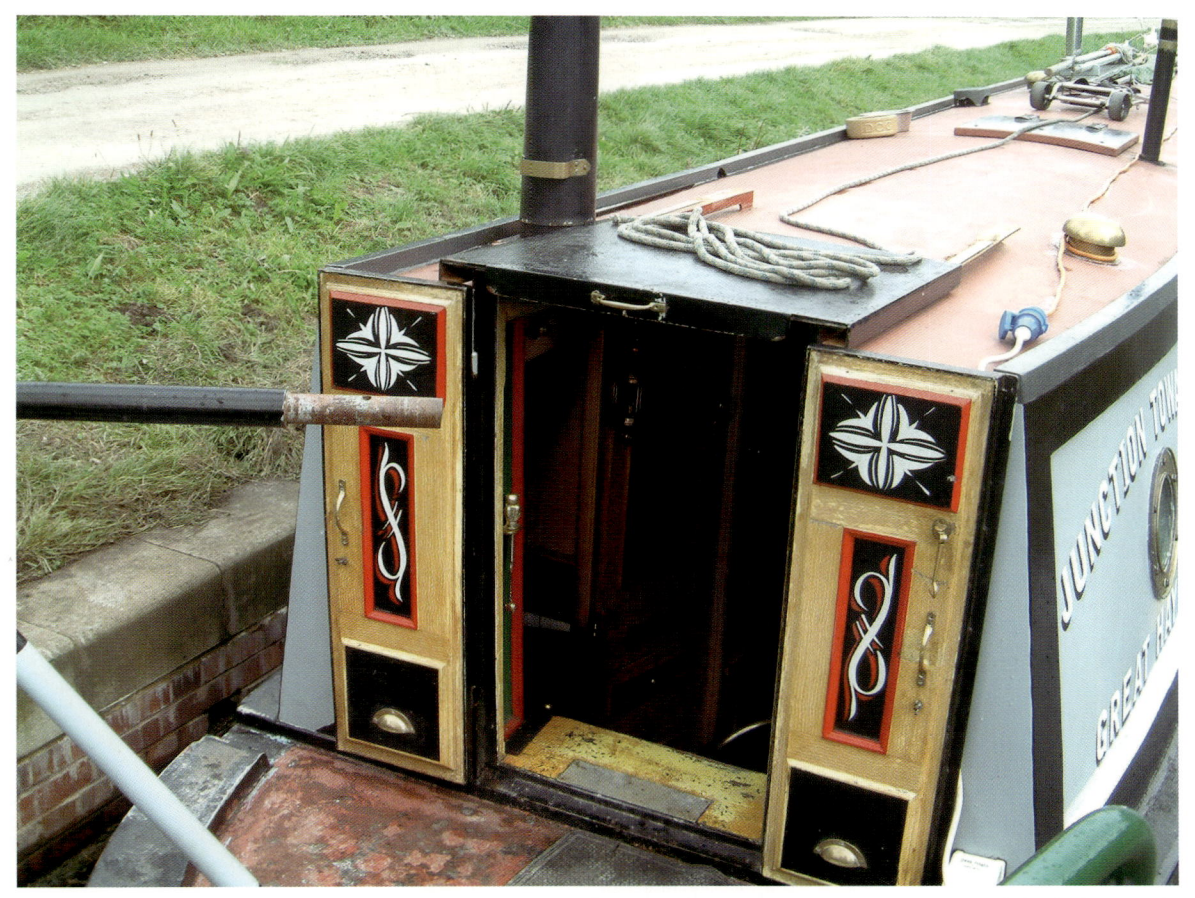

The back of a motor boat with the back doors open. The tiller has been removed as the craft is tied up and you can see the hole where the tiller pin slides through to prevent movement of the tiller while under way. Just to the left is the range, followed by the 'table cupboard', a cupboard where the door comes down to form a table. Lots of brass is in evidence.

You should see your surveyor as your best friend – they will draw your attention to what could be a problem at the next inspection and provide you with time to arrange for any large or expensive works.

Remember, there are two aspects to having your boat surveyed. You need to book a dry dock and a surveyor! Both may have long waiting lists so booking both early is advised.

CLEANING

One thing to remember is cleaning the outside of the boat. This again both adds a small amount to the cost of boat ownership and takes time, but you will want your boat to look spick and span and regular cleaning will prevent degradation of the superstructure. Hose down and use a soft cloth, then add polish (similar to cleaning a car – it just takes longer!). There is a lively debate about which polish is best to use.

Many boats have a stain running down from the bottom of the chimney. This is easy to remove if done on a regular basis but once it has built up it can become a major project.

If you have brasswork on the boat you will also need a constant supply of brass cleaning polish. Again, keeping your brass clean is not too difficult if

RUNNING COSTS

Constant greasing of the stern tube is vital. This unit sends grease down the pipe into the stern tube to keep water from trickling through it into the boat.

you do it regularly, but is a hard chore if only undertaken once in a while.

CONDENSATION

Condensation can be caused on a boat by many things. Human breath is one – you will be surprised how much water vapour is produced simply by breathing out.

While water heaters have to be vented outside the craft, gas hobs, kettles and cookers can put quite a bit of water vapour into the air, as can burning LPG.

Good internal cladding and insulation helps and good ventilation will stop most of the problem, but if you do have water vapour inside the boat it will settle somewhere cool such as the windows.

There are many dry docks around the system, some built from disused locks but most purpose-built, such as this one at Uxbridge. Part of the old FMC yard, this dock can take two boats side by side.

WATER INGRESS

Water inside the boat can come from a number of sources. The first possibility that comes to mind is a leak, which can be caused by pitting of the hull. Pits can occur both on the inside and outside of the hull. A good supply of anodes and a good coating of paint on a regular basis will prevent this. Other leaks can be caused by water dripping through the stern tube – and this can be prevented by keeping the tube well greased after each time you run your engine. Every so often the stern tube will need to be repacked to maintain the watertight seal and prevent damage to the prop shaft.

Condensation can cause a build-up of water in the bilges. This can accumulate in small quantities over time from a number of sources (*see above*).

Water can also come into the craft when working through locks, splashing over the gates into either end of the boat; it can also come out of the lock sides into open windows or hatches. A good example (at the time of writing) of a lock where you might pick up water in this way is the bottom lock in Buckby flight at Whilton.

Finally, when operating through tunnels, water can pour down the air shafts, so be careful to close hatches to prevent it from getting inside the craft.

These later examples will not flood your boat with large amounts of water, but over time it will build up in the bilges. In the long term this can lower the craft in the water and, in the worst situation, more water can then get into the boat via exhaust outlets and other hull fittings.

One common way to get a boat out of the water is on a slipway. This can either be lengthways or sideways. Most slipways are open to the elements but this one at Aylesbury is under cover. The boat is positioned on a pair of trolleys and guided towards the ramp until the bottom of the boat sits on the first trolley. It is then winched up the slip until it is out of the water.

DRY DOCKING

Every so often, your boat will need to come out of the water for underwater maintenance. While the boat is out of the water you can renew or top up the paint protection system, check for problems and commission a surveyor to inspect the underwater part of the hull (every six years).

You should plan this well in advance as most facilities for docking a boat are very booked up. There are three basic ways to do this.

The first is a **dry dock**. This operates in the same way as a lock but ends up with no water in the chamber to allow work to be carried out. The boat sits on 'dogs', or beams, so that most of the base plate is accessible. Some docks provided limited access under the craft.

The second way is to have the boat **slipped out.** Here a trolley is lowered into the water, the boat is positioned over the trolley and the two are guided towards the slip until the boat is sitting on the trolley, which is then hauled up the slip until the boat is clear of the water.

The final option is to have the boat lifted out by a crane and lowered onto – usually – a bed of old railway sleepers. This is the most common approach if there is a lot of work to be undertaken and the craft needs to be out for a long period, as the cost is often lower.

This is an ideal time to have a surveyor visit the craft to undertake a BSS inspection and check the hull. Again, forward planning is essential as surveyors get booked up.

Most modern narrow boats are constructed of mild steel plate welded to form both the hull and superstructure. Early craft had hulls made of wood (oak sides and elm bottoms); then the boat builders turned to riveted iron sides with elm bottoms; next came iron sides and bottoms, and finally steel. If you do own a riveted hull then you need to monitor the rivets to ensure that they have not worn out. Worn rivets can be replaced or welded over in dock.

The superstructure is, again, normally steel but there are examples of wood and GRP.

WET DOCKS

A wet dock is used by boat owners for such things as painting the outside of the boat. Many boat owners paint the superstructure in the open air and this is fine in good weather. At other times, painting the craft under cover is vital – you do not want rain on wet paint!

Painting any part of the boat requires sound preparation. You need to sand back the existing paintwork and start with undercoat (unless, of course, you have taken the sanding back to bare metal, in which case you need to start with a coat of oxide). This should be allowed to harden before adding another two coats of undercoat and at least two layers of the top coat. Finally, the lining and sign writing needs to be added, followed by the roses and castles and other decoration.

You can pick a boat out anywhere if you have a crane. Note the square of metal on which are hung the two slings that are passed under the craft. It is a legal requirement to have the crane inspected on a regular basis.

CHAPTER 7

DECORATION

The decoration of narrow boats is steeped in history and there are many books written on the subject (such as *Narrow Boat Painting* by A. J. Lewery).

Canal boat painting with the traditional roses and castles (as well as other designs) is believed to have started in the 1840s. It is thought that the idea came from the steerer and his family wanting to brighten up the craft that was their home. One steerer copied the ideas of another and so the standard designs took hold.

There are specialist firms along the canals who will undertake professional painting of your craft, including the signwriting and the traditional roses and castles.

If you are good at painting, you can undertake this work yourself, but the skill level required is high, and it is more common to have it done professionally.

BASIC PAINTING

If you do undertake the work yourself, you will need to obtain the correct paints and apply them in the right order.

A good-quality, professional paint job will last about ten to fifteen years if polished on a regular basis and if any scratches are treated and painted to prevent the steelwork rusting.

The rear of the Spirit *with the back doors open, showing the decoration on the doors and on the Buckby cans above.*

This boat is being rebuilt and a new back cabin is being constructed. There is no tiller and, judging by the height out of the water, there is no engine or ballast fitted. This is an ideal photo to show the bands painted round the stern. Most craft have red and white bands separated by black painted guards but there are many variations on the traditional theme.

It would be wrong to recommend any particular paint for two reasons. The first is that this is largely a matter of personal preference – and indeed, the different paint systems on the market all have groups of people who swear by them. The second reason, and perhaps the more important, is that paint systems are being improved all the time so the likelihood is that any comments I make here would soon be out of date.

What I would say is take advice both from other boat owners and from boatyards and boat painters.

Hull

There are two types of protective coating – black varnish (or bitumen), and two-coat epoxy resin. Black varnish is easier to apply and costs less. You would expect to apply at least three coats, allowing time to harden between each coat. The down side of black varnish is that it wears out in a few years and needs to be topped up on a regular basis. Craft in regular use need a fresh top coat every other year, and less frequently used craft every three or four years.

Two-coat epoxy is more expensive and the first time it is applied the hull needs to have just been sand- or grit-blasted. Not all docks allow this, so do check before you confirm the booking. The coating, once applied, should be topped up by a further two coats. A two-coat epoxy coating will give greater protection to the hull and will last much longer – in some cases up to twenty-five years!

One thing to stress is that you should not mix the two types! It is not too disastrous to put black varnish on top of two-coat but you should never put two-coat on top of black varnish. It is best to keep the two completely separate. Some boats are painted with two-coat below the bottom guard (the first 'rubbing straight' above the waterline) and black varnish above, as it is easier to top up.

Traditional painting dictates that the stern should be painted in two, sometimes three, bands. These are often red and white but other colours have been used. The theory is that these reflect lights from following craft in tunnels and in poor light, but this has become a standard way of painting the stern of a narrow boat.

While the boat is out of the water you can check the condition of your anodes, which are welded onto the hull to protect against corrosion (*see* Glossary). These waste away over time (which, of course, they are designed to do) and they may need replacing. I knew a boat owner once who painted the anodes with black varnish – not a good idea as it stops them working!

DECORATION

Do remember, if anyone is welding on your boat you should first of all disconnect the alternator to prevent damage.

Superstructure

The superstructure (or lid!) will, in most cases, extend for almost the full length of the boat. Starting from scratch, a good coat of oxide paint should be applied, followed by undercoat, which should be a marine or coach product.

The top coat should either be a marine paint or a coach varnish – there are many suppliers of these and you can often obtain them from the same source as the undercoat. Boatyards often supply only one product, however, so a search on the internet would give you more choice. Paint firms often have stands at rallies and boat shows so this is another good starting point.

Traditionally, boats have a two-colour paint system with lining separating the two colours. Such lining can be one or two colours in a thin line separating the two main colours. Lining out can be tricky and you should make sure that the main coat has fully dried and set hard before you try sticking masking tape on it!

ROSES AND CASTLES

This is the term given to the traditional designs painted on the outside of the cabins of narrow boats in carrying days. Back cabin doors would have fairy-tale castles painted on them with a stream running

On the Spirit *the engine room is at the stern, unlike on traditional craft, where the back cabin was at the back of the boat and the engine room forward of that. This photo shows the Buckby cans on the roof and the tiller in place on the swan's neck being held in position with the tiller pin. You can also see the exhaust stack topped by the cutter, the sign writing and painting of the back cabin doors and the bands round the back of the boat.*

underneath a bridge. Playing card symbols would be used and panels of roses, and sometimes other flowers, would brighten up both the boat cabin and equipment such as the Buckby can (used to carry drinking water), dippers and stools.

Many possible explanations have been given for the origins of the designs used. One theory is that Romany gypsies were employed to operate the craft and brought the designs with them though it seems more likely that it was only one steerer who painted his boat in the style and others simply copied. It seems that such designs were popular at the time. Another theory is that the designs were popular because they were easy to produce. All we can really know for certain is that all boats, for whatever reason, used the same style, or variations of it, for brightening up the craft that were both the workplace and home of the boat crews.

Today, classes are run in various parts of the canal system for those wishing to learn how to paint the various designs found on the craft, thus keeping the tradition alive.

At one time a series of transfers were produced but these were not up to the standard of individually painted images – I am not even sure if they are still available. I expect the problems were caused by the application rather than a defect in the product.

Another popular type of painting was 'scumbling'. This achieved a wood-grain look by painting the cabin side with cream paint and then covering this, once dry, with a coat of varnish. Before the varnish was dry a rubber comb was drawn through

The signwriting on the sides of the cabin on a working boat is a tradition that has been carried forward to modern craft.

the wet varnish, which created a pattern similar to wood grain, with the cream showing through where the comb had scraped the varnish away and leaving dark lines where the varnish had been left behind.

SIGNWRITING

Another tradition still going strong is the signwriting – much more difficult to master than the decorative paintwork. There are set type styles to use if you wish to keep to a traditional style, including Sans Serif, Ionic, Egyptian and Tuscan.

The boat owner would paint, or have painted, the name of the owner, the name of the boat and the home base on the sides of the craft as advertising. Some companies included the telephone number. It was an early form of advertising of course but even now at least half the narrow boats on the system still follow the historic trend (many with the original telephone number!).

In the 2000s, there are many variations on how a boat can be painted. One colour all over has been around for years of course, but today there are many artistic adaptations.

A number of narrow boats are left in oxide (bauxite or grey) and some are simply not painted, with rust showing through, which is very sad.

CHAPTER 8

WATERWORKS

WATER STORAGE

Water for drinking, washing and cooking was originally carried in water cans known as Buckby cans, which were kept on the cabin top. These were often gaily painted with roses and castles and were filled up from taps located at lock sides.

Modern craft have tanks for water storage, ranging in size from 20 to 200 gallons! These, of course, take much longer to fill up than a Buckby can, and over the years both the BWB and the CRT have moved water points away from the lock side to a point on the canal close to the lock so that a boat filling up with water is not blocking the lock while it replenishes its water supply.

A shower takes up less space than a bath and uses less water. The waste water needs to be pumped up to a suitable height above the waterline (10in).

If you are using a lockside tap, do not hold up other boaters. If another boat needs to use the lock, please just take enough water to keep you going and move on. You are never far from the next tap.

It is a good idea to sanitize or purify your water tank from time to time to prevent bugs from breeding in there and potentially giving you an upset stomach. You can buy purifiers in tablet form from most chandleries, and simply need to put a tablet in your tank each time you fill up. With some tablets, you may be advised not to drink the water for ten minutes after the tablet has been put in.

Should you have a stainless steel or plastic tank? A steel tank, suitably painted (with special paint!) inside to prevent rusting, is stronger but a plastic tank is of course lighter and easier to keep clean. Do make sure you can get inside to clean it from time to time. I have had both on *Spirit* and both did the job.

You will, of course, need a hose to connect to the tap at the water point to get the water into your tank. I would suggest you buy the 'crinkly' type, which stores far more easily, and get two 50ft (15m) lengths that can be joined together, along with different fittings for the tap end. Most CRT, EA and boatyard taps have a standard fitting but every so often you will find an old, non-standard, one. Most of the time you will find one 50ft length will serve but, every so often, you will find you need a longer hose. Make sure you use a food-quality hose.

PLUMBING

You should not use metal pipework for plumbing, as this will increase the risk of freezing in winter. The correct plastic pipe can be obtained from a chandlery with the correct fittings for joints and junctions.

A freshwater pump can be fitted in line between the water tank and the rest of the system. Do fit this with an on/off switch – you may need to switch the system off if you want to carry out alterations, such as adding a new tap, or in the event of a leak.

Sinks and showers can be emptied over the side, but remember an outlet needs to have a welded spigot on the inside and either be more than 10in (25cm) above the waterline, or protected to that height inside with an L-shaped spigot or a gate valve.

Bilge water and shower outlets can be pumped up to that level. Sinks can usually be emptied by gravity.

Some pumps are provided with screws so you can open them up. This is not a good idea on a regular basis, as the more often you take your pump apart, the greater the chance of damage to it when you put it back together.

Bath versus Shower

The question of whether to go for a shower or a bath is a personal choice.

A shower takes up less space but a bath can also be used for hand washing clothes and other purposes (such as washing pets!), and a bath at a suitable height can be emptied by gravity.

A bath at floor level or a shower have to have the water pumped out. An on/off switch here is a better option than a float switch (one more thing to go wrong).

Pumps

You will need a number of pumps on your boat, including one or two bilge pumps for pumping water that has found its way into the bilges. You can fit them with a float switch so that, in the event of the levels rising, the pump will automatically come on, switching off again when the float switch lowers. It is best also to have a switch in line, as float switches can go wrong.

Other pumps are needed to supply fresh water to the domestic water supply, empty showers and so on. They are usually very good quality, and you should get many years of satisfactory use out of such units.

Water Heating

In the days of carrying craft, water was heated in a kettle on the range. There was no running water and the water was stored in Buckby cans on the roof of the craft. These were filled up at taps situated at locks.

The normal way of providing hot water today is with a gas-operated water heater. This has to be vented correctly through the roof to prevent exhaust gas from escaping into the inside of the boat.

If the craft is not to be used in the winter months, it is vital to either drain the unit or flush out with pink antifreeze so the internal water pipes don't freeze in cold weather.

Many modern boats are able to heat water using a heat exchanger with the engine-cooling water to provide hot water.

Toilets

There are many toilet systems on the market but the main ones are the three described below.

The Elsan or 'bucket and chuck it' is a very basic system that is literally a bucket in which you put a fluid to deodorize the contents. This can then be emptied as required at the many sanitary stations on the waterway system. This is free, although some boatyards make a small charge.

This was the standard system used on craft (and indeed caravans and at campsites) until modern times. The unit was kept and used in the engine room.

Then there is the cassette-type system, such as a Porta Potti. Like the Elsan, it can be emptied at a sanitary station, but is built in two parts. A base tank holds the waste, while the top part, separated by a trapdoor, provides the seat. Flushing is provided by a separate tank that holds clean water to which one can add 'blue fluid' (sometimes green). This is a lot nicer to use but more difficult to clean!

One way to use an Elsan is to disguise it – on Spirit *an Elsan sits inside a specially built unit. Next to this, on the right, is the sink.*

Finally, you can have a loo that is connected to a holding tank. This system is far more like the sort of loo you would have at home, but there are two drawbacks: it costs money to pump the tank out, whether you do it yourself or to have it done for you, and the holding tank takes up space on the boat. Of course, the bigger the tank, the greater the time between pump-outs.

Before the 1960s, many boats simply deposited the contents over the side or had toilets (known as sea toilets) connected through outlets in the hull, but such units are now banned.

Over the years there have been a number of innovations brought out but none seem to have taken hold.

Washing Machines and Dishwashers

A few narrow boats and barges are fitted with one or both of these, especially residential craft. However, in order to operate such equipment, you need to have a supply of 230/240v mains electricity, either from a land line (in which case you need to have an RCD, or circuit-breaker, fitted), or from a generator or an inverter. However, you need to be careful not to create noise for other boaters and housing close to the canal in the first instance, and with an inverter you need to make sure you keep an eye on battery use. Normal domestic appliances as found at any normal retail outlet will work but do remember that you will be limited for space so size is important.

CHAPTER 9

EQUIPMENT

Unless you really know what you are doing, it is best to have equipment installed by a professional.

Most boatyards have a chandlery attached, some better stocked than others, and there are also a few specialist chandlers dotted around the system. Most will be pleased to give you practical advice and can assist you with any questions you may have.

If you do have gas on your boat it must be installed by a Gas Safe engineer. Gone are the days of DIY gas installations!

NAVIGATION EQUIPMENT

Windlasses

To navigate the canal system you will need windlass handles (shortened to windlasses) to raise and lower the paddles at locks. You need at least two standard ones and a long-handled one to tackle stiff paddle gear. In the old days you needed different windlasses for different canals, then in the 1970s, double-headed versions were produced with two of the more common spindle sizes side by side (or one above the other). The BWB and CRT have, over the years, standardized the spindle size and a tapered spindle hole caters for the rest. Most windlasses are steel but some are produced in gunmetal or brass, although brass ones are a bit too soft for general use.

If you have a double-headed windlass, make sure you use the correct hole to avoid damage to the spindle. A slipping windlass can also cause injury to the user.

You will need one or two shafts on the roof to help push the boat off a shallow part if required, and a cabin shaft, which is about 6ft (2m) long and has a point and hook at the end. This is kept in reach of the steerer and is used for hooking things out of the canal and pushing the back of the boat away from lock sides.

You will also need fenders at both front and stern (be careful not to get either your rudder or the fender caught in the mitre of the gates!), as well as ropes and chains.

Fenders should be fitted with a weak link, which you can create by hacksawing through a link in the chain holding the fender on. This is a safety measure. If your fender gets caught in a gate it will come off rather than lifting the gate or sinking your boat.

Anchors

An anchor will be needed if you intend to venture onto rivers, even non-tidal ones!

An anchor is required if you intend to take your narrow boat off the canals and onto a river. It should be kept at the 'uphill' end of the craft and ready for use.

Should you get into difficulty (such as an engine failure) you can drop the anchor over the side which should hold you and save you from being swept away out of control. I prefer to have the anchor at the 'uphill' end of my boat so that if I do have to use it, I do not find my boat trying to swing round in the flow.

The anchor should be connected to the craft with a length of chain and then rope. The weight of the anchor, and length of chain and rope, will depend on the length of your boat (and thus the weight of the boat); your local boatyard will help you here. The depth of water you are travelling through will also need to be taken into account – obviously, the deeper the water the longer line you will need!

A mud weight is also a good idea. This is (usually) a 56lb weight with a rope attached that you can drop over the side to keep one end of your boat in place. It is not always possible to tie up alongside and you may have to put your bow or stern in and tie up one end of your boat, leaving the other end 'flapping'. This is not as secure as tying up, but will keep your boat in roughly the position you want it.

Access Key

You will also need to obtain from the CRT a key to access the sanitary stations along the canal system and to operate some swing bridges and open gates onto the towing path. It is also used on CRT anti-vandal devices on locks (a sort of handcuff on the spindle). The key can also be used for access to other areas, such as boatyards. Always remember to lock up after yourself!

Ropes

You can never have too many ropes. These are used for a number of purposes; the obvious example is tying up the boat, but they can also help in pulling the craft to the bank and towing, among other functions.

Most ropes are about 30ft (9m) long and are called straps. These normally have an eye splice at one end only. The canal term 'to strap off' means to hold the boat by taking a strap round something, usually a bollard, to hold the boat from going forward (or back).

Other ropes found on a working boat (that can also come in useful on a modern boat) are a long rope about 70ft (21m) long (called a snubber), which would be used for towing on a long line or helping to bring the butty into a lock on a narrow canal; and two short (6–8ft/2–2.5m) lengths with an eye splice at each end for towing close up. These are called cross straps and are used to keep the bow of the boat being towed close up to the stern of the towing boat. Normal practice is to have an empty butty on cross straps and a loaded one on a long line.

Having mentioned towing on a long line (used where there is a good distance between locks) and close up, this is a good point to mention the third method of pairing up a motor and butty: side by side or 'breasted up'. Here the two craft are tied up bow to bow. This method is often used in lock flights (wide locks, of course) or locations where locks are close together. The two boats are tied tightly together and effectively become one unit.

Horns

It is a requirement that your craft is fitted with an audible device to warn other craft of your approach. The horn can also be used to send sound signals to other craft (*see below*), and it is a good idea to know the sound signals.

It is a very good idea to have a hand-held audible device in addition to the normal 12v or 24v fitted version. The main horn can go wrong for a number of reasons.

Headlights

Known as 'tunnel lamps', a light is required at the bow to show the position of the craft in tunnels. Some craft these days are fitted with twin halogen lamps, but this is not advisable as it can look like a pair of boats rather than one boat coming towards you.

You should also remember that the purpose of a headlight is to show a boat coming towards you where you are, not to blind the steerer!

Again, having a back-up on board, such as a powerful torch, is a good idea. As with the tunnel lamp, be careful where the beam is pointed.

Roof

Some boats are fitted with pram hoods (which can drop down) or even fixed structures over the back deck. While these provide a degree of protection when it is raining, they can also cause a problem when going under low bridges. I discovered that the highest point on my roof, with the cans moved inside, is my tiller pin. I took it off going into Stratford Basin in 1990 and had to spend a couple of days with a screwdriver in its place!

The roof of your boat is not somewhere to keep cycles, logs, baskets of flowers or anything else that might stop you seeing ahead, get stolen or be swept off by a passing tree! I saw a boat once with a garden centre on the roof, which was swept along the roof by an overhanging branch and down onto the back deck just as Mrs Boat Owner came out of the back doors to find out what the noise was. She was not happy.

Using your roof as a storeroom also risks damaging your paintwork or making the boat unstable. It should have on it one or two poles or shafts, a mooring plank and one or two water or Buckby cans and that is it!

INTERNAL EQUIPMENT

Heating Systems

Most boats are fitted with coal/wood stoves. These are either simple enclosed fires or have a back boiler fitted, which, in turn, heats water to supply a number of radiators. While boats fall outside the provisions of the Clean Air Act, burning coal and wood will perhaps upset those round you, such as other boat owners and local residents. Smokeless fuel is readily available from garages and local stores.

There are many coal boats on the system that can

A boat roof should be kept clear except for shafts and, at the rear, Buckby cans. Using the boat roof for storage of coal, cycles and flowerpots is not a good idea as they can cause a trip hazard.

EQUIPMENT

A solid fuel fire needs to be protected from surrounding woodwork, including the chimney, to avoid setting fire to the craft in the event of overheating.

supply coal and smokeless fuel, and often red diesel and Calor gas (LPG) as well.

When fitting a fire it is vital to protect the surrounding woodwork from the heat. Boats have caught fire because a stove overheated.

There are other methods of heating such as diesel heaters and gas – although the latter can cause condensation on older craft and is not ideal. Mobile heaters with a gas cylinder inside are not allowed on a boat and you should not even consider such units.

Cooking

The normal method of cooking on a boat is a gas cooker fitted to a cylinder in a gas-tight locker. A good marine chandler will be able to supply you with a suitable device that will run either on butane or propane. You can heat a kettle on top of a coal stove.

Some boats are fitted with diesel hobs and some cook on a small range, although these are both rare.

Gas

As mentioned above, any gas appliances have to be installed by a Gas Safe engineer. You used to be able to instal gas piping yourself and have the work checked by the engineer after installation but it is no longer possible to do this.

The gas is supplied from a cylinder, which is stored in a gas-tight locker with a vent over the side in case a leak happens. It is normal to have room in your locker to store two cylinders, one being a spare; you do not want to run out of gas in the middle of cooking Sunday lunch (done that!). There are two types of gas available, butane or propane. Most boats are fitted with propane which will still operate in cold weather (unless it gets really cold!) although some boats do use butane. Butane bottles do not provide a good supply of gas in cold conditions.

Gas can be used for cooking, running a fridge (if already installed) and heating (not advised). You are not now allowed to fit a boat with a gas fridge, but an existing installation is acceptable in a craft built prior to 1998.

My boat was also fitted with gas lights in the

EQUIPMENT

LPG gas needs to be stored in a gas-tight locker, which can vent overboard in the event of a leak. Generators need to be kept in a similar container.

1970s but we replaced them with 12v electric ones in the early 80s.

Firefighting

Your firefighting equipment is a requirement of the BSS, and should not be overlooked. If your boat is over 36ft (11m) long you need a minimum of three 5A34B rated extinguishers with a total rating of 21A144B on the boat. Shorter craft have lower requirements.

Such equipment should be checked by a qualified person on a regular basis, although for some reason this is not, at the time of writing, a requirement of the BSS. Dry powder extinguishers may need to be refilled with powder and have the CO_2 bulb replaced. Modern dry powder units have a small valve on them and, if not under enough pressure, they can be refilled; a supplier will not do this if the unit is out of date, however – about ten years after being made (they have a date stamp on the casing).

CO_2 extinguishers, which are not listed by the BSS, need to be refilled. It is easier, but more expensive, simply to replace the units. A CO_2 extinguisher will last ten years and simply has to be weighed to be checked – if it's under weight, refill it. I mention CO_2 extinguishers, even though they are not BSS listed, as they are clean and can put out most fires. The BSS does not list them as they are not rated for putting out wood fires.

Foam is another type of extinguisher permitted under the BSS inspection but these are somewhat on the large side.

Once upon a time the colour of an extinguisher indicated what it contained – black for CO_2, blue for dry powder, cream for foam and so on. All fire extinguishers now have to be red. Also once upon a time, halon gas fire extinguishers were recommended (these were green) but they are now banned as they produce a dangerous gas, which, in the confines of a narrow boat cabin, can be lethal.

The larger unit is a CO_2 extinguisher, which used to be painted black, and the smaller one is a dry powder one, which used to be blue. Now all extinguishers are red.

It is a requirement of the Boat Safety Scheme that the craft carries a fire blanket as well as fire extinguishers.

You will also be required to have a fire blanket in the galley.

Having the units checked on a regular basis is not that expensive and should form part of your ongoing maintenance although, as mentioned above, the BSS inspection does not check on this. For your own peace of mind it is a good idea to have them checked every few years.

Alarms

For your protection while on board, you may wish to consider installing some or all of the following alarms. I put it in these terms, as neither your insurers nor the navigation authorities seem to require them on private pleasure craft. I say 'while on board' because an alarm going off on an empty boat may or may not draw attention to the situation to others outside – the obvious exception here is if the boat is moored in a marina.

A **gas alarm** will alert you to a gas leak on board. Such leaks are rare today compared with the 1960s and 70s due to the more stringent requirements of the Gas Safe scheme (previously CORGI), flame failure devices and so on.

A **CO alarm** will alert you to carbon monoxide being present and is perhaps the most important alarm to have as carbon monoxide is hard to detect without one. Not for nothing has it been described as the silent killer! An increase in the level of CO can make people on board fall asleep and not wake up. It can be caused by a leak of CO from a solid fuel stove or gas water-heater, coupled with a lack of ventilation.

A **smoke alarm** will alert you to smoke being present (or the fact that you are cooking bacon!), which, in turn, could lead to fire. If you are on board asleep the alarm can wake you up in time to attend to the fire or escape from the boat.

A **burglar alarm** in itself is perhaps not much help, as a boat going past too fast can set it off. Pressure pads are better, but if you are not on the boat, who will take note of the alarm going off? You can now install surveillance cameras that will send a live video feed to your smartphone of the inside of your boat, so that if someone does break in, you can record their actions and provide a copy to the police. You may even be lucky enough to get the police to attend while the robber is still on board.

Electricity

A 12v or 24v system can supply lighting and is one way to run a fridge. It is also useful to fit sockets into which to plug chargers and other equipment.

Most equipment (such as mobile phone chargers) these days can run off a 12v system. There will

You need to have the correct plug to connect with the 12v system on your boat.

normally be a 12v system on the boat for engine starting and internal lighting so it is a good idea to use this system for recharging as well.

See Chapter 10 for more on electrics.

TV

A portable television can be run if it has a 12v input but be aware that it will run your domestic battery down, and you will often find it difficult to get a signal. There are companies that can supply a dish to put on the roof of the boat, but you have to reposition it each time you moor up. They do seem to be becoming more and more popular nonetheless.

Mobile Phones and Internet

If you are trying to use a mobile phone inside your boat, remember that you are in a steel box so you might not get a good signal – or any signal at all! Standing by a window will help, or go outside and stand on the bow or stern. Regardless of your service provider, you will find some locations where you are not able to get a signal at all.

If you have 12v DC electricity then charging will not be a problem – just like in your car.

Many people like to get away from the rest of the world on their boat, while others like to keep in touch. In the latter case you need to talk to your service provider about the best way to connect your laptop or tablet to the outside world. One way to connect to the internet is to obtain a dongle that plugs into your mobile or laptop and connects you to the web via a mobile telephone signal.

Technology in this field moves on swiftly, so do your research before going ahead with a purchase. You can always find access to the internet somewhere on your journey.

It is normal to install a 12v TV on a boat where the domestic DC voltage is 12v.

Windows

Windows supplied to boat owners and boatyards normally come from specialist companies. It is possible to obtain windows from other sources: as an example, in 1975 my boat was fitted with second-hand bus windows and these are still there, although two have been replaced, one by a door and the other by a porthole.

If you are buying windows make sure the units can have the glass replaced easily.

Security needs to be a consideration. Make sure that your windows do not open wide enough for an intruder to get through. Some people like to have a large opening in the summer that can be kept open whilst they are going along. This is fine but do make sure your boat cannot be broken into – perhaps by fitting a grille or shutter over the opening when the boat is left unattended.

CHAPTER 10

ELECTRICS

Most boats have either a 12v or 24v DC system fitted to provide engine start, lighting and other power supply requirements.

Thin wire is a big no-no as this can overheat and start a fire. If you are undertaking installation of or repairs to DC wiring yourself then make sure you get professional advice regarding the type of wire to use. The thicker the wire the better, as this will prevent voltage loss at the end farthest from the battery.

You will need at least two colours of insulation – black and red are normal – and never use the hull as a negative return as this can cause a number of problems, such as electrolysis through the hull.

Because a starter motor needs a quick spurt of high energy and your domestic system will require a constant low amperage supply over a long period, you need two separate battery systems – one starter battery to start the engine and one or more domestic batteries. Your engine will put electricity back into the batteries via an alternator. It is important to separate this supply with a split charging system so that the starter battery is not drained into the domestic system – you will need to start the engine to recharge the domestic batteries if they run down.

Batteries must be stored in a box with a non-conductive lid. This is to prevent items falling onto the battery terminals and shorting out. You can get a nice big spark which, in turn, can cause a fire.

You also need to check that the terminals are tight. Vibration can cause them to work loose.

12 OR 24 VOLTS

Most craft are fitted with a 12v direct current system. Most engine starters are 12v and there is far more 12v equipment on the market (although more and more 24v equipment is becoming available). The advantage of 24v is that the higher voltage means your system is less affected by voltage loss, which could be important in a full-length boat. Voltage loss occurs when the power has to travel down long lengths of wire. Using thicker wire is another way to keep voltage loss to a minimum.

Batteries should be kept in a battery box with a non-conductive lid.

ELECTRICS

Some boats are fitted with a mains system to charge batteries on board. The connection is a marine connection but it is a good idea to have a 13 amp converter in case you need to charge up from a standard domestic supply.

Nonetheless, the ready availability of 12v equipment on the high street means that the greater majority of boats are still fitted with a 12v system. This means the equipment you use in your car can also be used in your boat.

It is important to have one or two battery isolator switches fitted. One will cut off all the 12v or 24v power to the entire boat. If you have two, one will cut off the domestic supply and the other will cut off the supply to the starter motor on the engine.

Most batteries today are maintenance-free, but there are still some around where you need to top up the distilled water and this needs to be checked on a regular basis – every two or three months, or more often if the craft is in constant use.

MAINS

There are two reasons why you would have mains (220–240 volt alternating current) on your boat and three ways to supply it. It all depends on what you hope to do with it and where you are at the time.

The main reason you would need mains is to run 220–240v equipment. For short periods you can use an inverter. This converts 12v (or 24v) DC to 240v AC to run electrical items but this will drain the batteries. You can, of course, mitigate this by using such a system with the engine running. As an example, a washing machine can be used during the day while boating. Watching a mains television at night would cause a problem, however, unless you were moored out in the country where your engine noise would not upset other boat owners or nearby residents.

You can use a generator but remember that even the 'quiet' versions can have the same effect as running your engine to those around you. Such a unit is useful if you are moored up in the middle of nowhere and you get up in the morning to find your engine will not start for one reason or another. Another good point is that you can get the generator out anywhere and run it to provide power for such things as power tools if you need to carry out emergency work, but do bear in mind the point regarding your neighbours. When running an engine or generator, the sound can be amplified by bouncing off the surface of the water and thus the noise will be louder to someone on the other side of the canal than to you. Many modern craft are built with on-board silent generators that run on diesel.

ELECTRICS

Generators, together with any spare fuel (normally petrol but diesel and gas versions do exist), must be stored in a gas-tight locker when kept on board out of use.

It is normal to run generators on the towpath, which can be a security risk unless they are fixed to the craft by chain and padlock. Do check this point with your Insurer and make sure the item is listed on the schedule.

The final way to get mains onto your boat is via a land line, which, of course, only helps if you are moored at a location with mains power. This might be on your home mooring or at a boatyard you are visiting that can supply a hook-up.

In all situations you must ensure that your system has an earth leak circuit breaker or residual circuit device trip and mini circuit breaker built into the wiring system. Water and electricity do not mix! You can buy plugs with a circuit breaker or galvanic isolators built in and they are not expensive. Most canalside facilities provide power through round waterproof sockets. It is a good idea to have both types of leads.

Canalside mains supply is standard in marinas but can also be found elsewhere.

CHAPTER 11

ENGINES

While there are various types of craft designed without engines (such as butties, horse boats, day boats and the like) the vast majority of narrow boats and barges are fitted with one. Over 95 per cent of the time, this will be a diesel engine.

The speed of the craft is not simply a product of the horsepower of the engine but a combination of the torque, the gearbox and the size of the propeller.

The torque, simply put, is the power with which the engine turns the prop shaft. The gear box is normally one of three systems – direct drive, two to one or three to one. These transfer the power from the engine to the prop shaft at the same speed, half the speed or a third of the speed of the engine. The size of the propeller will affect the speed at which water is drawn down the swim and thrust out of the back of the boat, pushing the boat forward in the water.

It is important to get all three of these components set up optimally for your boat. A marine engineer can work it all out for you.

TYPES OF ENGINE

Diesel

The vast majority of craft, as mentioned above, are equipped with diesel engines. A 70ft (21.3m) narrow boat will be quite happy with a 24hp two-cylinder engine if it is installed correctly.

Most diesel engines these days are four-cylinder but many boat owners prefer two- or three-cylinder units.

ENGINES

Such an engine will need cooling and there are three ways to achieve this:

Air cooling requires a flow of air, drawn from outside the boat.

Raw water cooling takes water from the canal via a 'mud box' to ensure that the system is not clogged with mud and silt, leading to overheating.

Closed water or 'skin tank/keel' cooling works by passing water round the engine, where it is heated, and then back to a thin tank fitted to the swim or underwater side of the craft, where it cools with contact with colder water in the canal.

Some engines fitted to narrow boats are described as 'marine engines' but most are either generator engines or units that would be just as happy in a tractor or van.

Single-, twin-, three- and four-cylinder engines are all in use and, every so often, you will find a six-cylinder unit. The average unit is rated at between 20 and 30 horsepower although higher HP engines are sometimes used.

Semi-Diesel

The 'semi-diesel' or 'heavy oil' engine was the first kind of diesel engine to be fitted to narrow boats and quickly replaced steam engines, which, with boiler and fuel, took up too much valuable hold space. A number of these engines are still in use and, in the main, are 9 or 15hp. Most are Bolinder engines and were fitted to FMC craft in the early 1890s.

Early models had to be started with a blow lamp and a kick on the fly wheel, and changing from forward to reverse was a challenge. This is definitely an engine for the enthusiast!

Petrol and TVO

Petrol and TVO (tractor vaporizing oil) engines are rare and becoming rarer as time passes. They are fitted in the same way as a diesel unit.

Outboards

Outboards are designed for use on cruisers and other small craft but some narrow boats were built with an outboard housing welded to the back. Outboards have also been fitted to butty boats, either on a bracket again welded to the rear of the

Original Bolinder engines were 9hp units but this is an example of a larger 15hp version.

craft to one side of the rudder, or fitted to the rudder itself.

An outboard can either be connected to a wheel in the craft or the boat can be steered using the inbuilt handle on the unit. There are both petrol and diesel versions in use.

Gas

There was a move in the 1970s and 80s to fit narrow boats with petrol engines converted to run on LPG (liquefied petroleum gas). I understand that these have now all been removed and replaced by diesel units, as they were considered to be unsafe.

An outboard engine on a GRP (glass reinforced plastic) cruiser.

The steam motor boat President *with its normal butty,* Kildare*, in a lock. You may be able to see the longer engine room, which is home to the boiler and steam engine. This took up cargo space and canal companies quickly switched to diesel power when such units became available.*

Electric

Electric engines are more often found fitted to GRP (glass reinforced plastic) cruisers and there are many examples of this type of unit. Only a few narrow boats were so fitted due to the lower power output.

One recent idea is to run an electric engine using solar panels – I recently saw such a boat moored on the towpath opposite my wharf.

Hydraulic Drive

In the 1980s and 90s, hydraulic drive engines looked to be the propulsion method of the future, but now seem to have disappeared. I have not heard of such a unit for the last fifteen years or so, although the odd unit may still be out there.

Steam

As mentioned above, the move from horse-drawn to self-propelled craft was first tried with steam engines. The problem was the space taken up by the boiler and the storage of fuel. Most steam-driven craft were converted to diesel, but there are examples of both ex-working craft and modern craft so fitted. I even know about a hire boat that was fitted with a steam engine.

The best-known steam-powered narrow boat using the system today is *President*, an ex-FMC boat.

Hydrogen

The hydrogen engine is a modern concept, which has been fitted to one boat at least. This type of unit

The modern way of controlling the boat's speed and direction is via a Morse control. Most cruiser-stern narrow boats are fitted with such an arrangement.

may start to catch on as the main issue was the cost of the fuel cells, which have now come down in price dramatically.

This unit could be the future.

Bow Thrusters

Modern narrow boats are sometimes fitted with bow thrusters. This system is a tube going across the bow of the boat underwater with an electric propeller, operated from the stern, in the middle of the tube. This can assist with moving the bow out in certain situations. However, I have witnessed many situations where a bow thruster was used when not required, and sometimes when using it actually hindered what the steerer was trying to do!

These are powered either by 12v or 24v or by hydraulic units.

ALIGNMENT

Whatever type of engine you have, it is important to have the unit lined up correctly with the prop shaft and stern tube.

It will, of course, have been lined up correctly at installation but it can move out of alignment over time, which causes wear on both the propeller and the stern tube.

A speed wheel controls how fast the engine is running. Turn it clockwise to speed the engine up and anticlockwise to slow down. Separate to this is the gear lever, which has three positions – forward, reverse and neutral.

A control panel has a number of items grouped on it. The oil pressure gauge is the most important. Other items include battery charging indicators, temperature gauge and switches to operate the horn, tunnel light, bilge pump and other electrical items you may have installed.

If you have your engine serviced by a boatyard, you can ask them to check the unit at the same time. If you undertake your own service then it is a good idea to call in at a boatyard separately to have the engine alignment checked.

ENGINE CONTROLS

You can either have a modern Morse control (named after the original manufacturer), which provides acceleration and gears in one unit, or use a more traditional method.

On a Morse control there is a button to push in if you wish to rev the engine without engaging the gear.

A traditional arrangement separates the two, and you will have a gear lever and (normally) a speed wheel, which is turned to increase or decrease the speed of the engine.

Your engine control panel will also include such items as an oil pressure gauge, a battery charging indicator and an engine temperature gauge, as well as indicator lights and switches to operate your tunnel lamp, horn, bilge pump and, if fitted, your bow thruster.

You may also have a battery management system fitted and this will add to the indicator lamps. This will make sure that your batteries are charged (but not overcharged) and kept at optimum performance.

ENGINE MAINTENANCE

Because most narrow boats are fitted with diesel engines, I will restrict this section to the maintenance of such units. Much of the information below, however, applies to many of the engine types listed above.

First of all, there are things you need to keep in the engine room or somewhere else on the boat:

- A spare drive belt – make sure it is the correct one for the drive wheels on your engine, as the wrong one will not work. Drive belts can be used in the engine room to transfer power from the engine to other equipment, such as an alternator
- Fuel and air filters – have a couple of each of these on hand
- Injectors – these can go wrong and a spare one for each cylinder is always a good idea (I know from personal experience!)
- Oil – always carry a drum of engine oil
- Stern tube grease
- Fuses

Your maintenance routine should include the following as a minimum:

- Daily (when boating): grease the stern tube at the end of each day.
- Monthly: check the oil levels in both the engine and the gearbox (more often if the craft is in constant use).
- Depending on the cruising undertaken but never less than once a year: change the filters and oil.

Another thing that needs to be checked every so often is the condition of the fuel pipes. Old fuel pipes can, with engine vibration and other causes, allow fuel leaks and/or let air into the fuel supply to the engine.

FUEL TANKS

In most narrow boats, the amount of diesel in the tank will vary. When the level is low, you can get

The dipstick sits in a pipe that guides the stick into the sump. This should be checked on a regular basis to ensure that the engine has enough oil in it to protect the moving parts.

condensation forming on the underside of the top of the tank, which will end up in the fuel along with other muck that will collect at the bottom of the tank.

Of course, you will have a fuel filter fitted, which will stop all or most of the rubbish from getting into your engine and damaging it. If your tank is low in fuel, however, and for some reason your tank is churned up (for example when passing other craft on a wide waterway and bouncing on their wash), the rubbish that usually lies at the bottom of the tank could end up feeding into the fuel pipe to the engine and block the fuel filter, which, of course, will stop the engine.

Most tanks do have a lower level below the fuel out-take where this muck will normally stay, but every so often you need to have it cleaned out. This is a job for a boatyard, who will pump out any 'good' fuel (and put it back later!) and then clean out the bottom of the tank.

It should also be remembered that modern diesel has a percentage of biofuel in it, so you need to put an additive in the tank to stop bacterial growth (diesel bug), which is a problem associated with biodiesel. This can be purchased from your local boatyard or chandlery.

Some boats have a 'bulk' fuel tank low down in the hull with a pump to pass the fuel up to a 'day tank' high up above the engine, from where it feeds down to the engine by gravity. If you have a boat with such a system you must fill the day tank each morning before setting off.

EXHAUST SYSTEM

Regardless of the position of the exhaust (out of the side or through the roof), you need to make sure that the pipework is properly protected by a heatproof bandage, as it can get very hot and could injure anyone coming into contact with it.

With many modern craft, such as cruiser-stern boats, the exhaust comes out of the side of the boat close to the engine. On working boats, which could be loaded to the point where the exhaust, if passed through the side, would end up underwater, this would have been impossible, so the exhaust passed through the roof with a short chimney taking the blast away from the steerer. The top is fitted with a circle of metal (normally brass) called a cutter.

CHAPTER 12

WHEN THINGS GO WRONG

All sorts of misfortunes can affect your cruise – often caused by you failing to concentrate on the job in hand – which, of course, is why you take out an insurance policy. Serious damage is rare, but every so often one does hear of major losses, including, sadly, occasional loss of life.

If your boat is involved in an incident, you should advise your insurance provider as soon as possible. In the event of a serious problem they may appoint a surveyor to assist in recovery and repair.

I stress that such situations are rare, and keeping alert will prevent all or many of the problems you could have.

BREAKING DOWN

This is very likely to happen to you at some point, and when it does you are bound to be miles from the nearest boatyard.

Elsewhere in this book I have listed the more common items you need to carry as spares. You will also, of course, need a toolbox containing a set of spanners with one or two adjustable ones, various screwdrivers, pliers, side cutters, a knife, a hacksaw and a hammer. A club hammer and a set of bolt croppers will occasionally come in handy, as will a pair of secateurs to trim overhanging branches. Other useful items are PTFE tape, fuses and a selection of jubilee clips.

Even with all this, unless you are good with engines, it is a good idea to have River Canal Rescue (RCR) membership, either directly or through your insurance policy.

In the 1970s and 80s a number of breakdown companies were started, but they never lasted. Some offered a good service but in a restricted area, while others were simply a call centre who would call out a local boatyard.

It was not until River Canal Rescue came along that we got a national system on our inland waterways that worked. Some insurers now offer the RCR

RCR (River Canal Rescue) attend members' craft when they break down and will either fix the problem or tow the boat to their home marina.

service as an add-on to their policies but often you have to pay for each call-out. Direct membership also includes provision of replacement parts but if you have an 'unusual' engine you might have to wait while they source the needed part so it's best to carry your own (see above).

SINKING

A sinking is not a total disaster, although it is of course very distressing. The biggest problem is the fact that everything gets wet! The boat itself can be raised, dried and repaired.

The worst issue is the tidemark of oil and blue fluid on the woodwork inside the boat, so it may need replacing. Fridges will need to be thrown out, as will other electrical goods, such as televisions, and anything made of paper. The rest can basically be dried out, although woodwork may become distorted, even if it escapes staining.

One thing to remember is that the engine must be flushed through with oil as soon after raising as possible. Being underwater will not in itself cause that much damage to an engine, but as soon as it is lifted out and air can mix inside with the water, rust will start to form very quickly.

Causes

There are many reasons why a boat might sink. As far as the boat itself is concerned, there are a number of points at the rear of the craft that can cause a problem: the stern tube, the weed hatch, intake for water-cooled engines and exhaust outlets where these go through the hull.

If the craft is fitted with a hull outlet for the engine exhaust, then the outlet may, if the craft tilts over, allow water to pour into the back of the craft, resulting in sinking by the stern. Ex-working boats had the exhaust coming out through the roof so this could not happen.

Failure of the plumbing for water intakes causes the same problem but can happen at any time. In cold conditions, for example, water in the system can freeze, splitting the pipes, which, when thawed, will allow water to enter the craft.

Another modern problem, because working boats were not fitted with weed hatches, is starting the engine with the weed hatch cover off or badly refitted. This is the quickest way to sink a boat! A weed hatch is great if you get 'propped up', as it allows

There are many reasons why disaster can strike in a lock. The most common is catching the boat on the lock cill.

WHEN THINGS GO WRONG

A weed hatch is found on modern craft and enables the owner to gain access to the propeller to free rubbish caught round it. The quickest way to sink a boat is to start the engine in gear with the weed hatch off or incorrectly fitted.

easy access to the propeller to remove any offending material that has wound itself round the shaft and/or the propeller itself, but great care must be taken over reassembling the protective cover before starting the engine.

The final boat-related possibility is water dripping through the stern tube. This will happen slowly over a period of time, until the stern gets to the point where an exhaust or bilge pump outlet is brought down to water level and then the water pours in and the craft sinks.

Forward of the engine area there are not too many problems, although outlets through the hull pose the same potential problems as at the stern. Thinning of steelwork can, over the years, result in an area where the plating will not hold if hit by another craft or if the craft comes into contact with the infrastructure of the waterway.

Locks

Perhaps the likeliest cause of sinking is a mistake made in a lock. You should always be aware of what is happening to your boat in a lock, as disaster can strike very quickly if you take your eye off the ball. While it is possible to refloat a boat in a lock, it often needs a crane to lift it out.

The number of craft sinking in locks has risen over the past few years, which, I suggest, is due to a combination of ignorance of how locks work, and not paying enough attention.

WHEN THINGS GO WRONG

The top lock gates sit on a cill, which is the bottom of the canal at the upper level. The unwary can catch the stern of their boat on this cill and damage it and, in the worst situation, can cause the boat to turn over and/or sink. Always keep the back of the boat well away from the cill – usually where it is will be marked on the side of the lock.

The most common scenario is when a boat gets 'hung up' when going downhill – that is, when the stern becomes stuck on the cill that protrudes underneath the back gates as the water flows out.

In a wide lock, the craft can twist and nosedive; this can happen even in a narrow lock if it is deep enough. Again, when locking down, if you tie the craft up the water will run away but the craft will stay where it is until the rope breaks under the strain and the craft crashes down and may sink.

The bow or bow fender can get trapped in the gate (which is why it is a good idea to have a weak link) – this can happen going up or down in the lock, although more often going up. It is important to remember not to open gate paddles until the decks are above the level of the water otherwise you can flood the boat, which can result in sinking or at least cause severe damage.

You can also catch the sacrificial chine on brickwork on the side of the lock wall. This will normally result in the craft leaning over and it will then right itself. Such a situation will not often lead to a disaster but it can happen.

Do keep aware of the trim of the boat while going up or down in a lock and, if you do get caught, keep your finger on the horn and shout 'Drop the paddles' – keep shouting it until those at the lock gates take in what is wrong and take action.

Never leave your boat going up or down in a lock to go off to do something else. If you do and something does go wrong, there will be no one there to realize that there is a problem and able to take action to resolve it.

On a river you should, of course, keep well away from weirs!

On tidal waterways do bear in mind that the water will go up and down and your boat will try to go up and down with it – make sure it can!

Prevention

As most of these problems arise in the last 10ft (3m) of the craft, the fitting of a watertight bulkhead between the engine area and the hold will prevent the craft from sinking if things go wrong. You will still have to deal with a flooded engine room but at least the boat will stay afloat and the inside and contents should escape damage.

If you take the weed hatch off then it essential to make sure that the engine has been turned off first and is not started again until the weed hatch is refitted and has been checked. One boat sank because the weed hatch cover had been put on back to front and this went unnoticed.

Greasing the stern tube at the end of each boating session should prevent water from getting down that way, although it is wise to have this repacked on a regular basis.

When working through a lock, make sure you do not have any ropes ashore which will prevent the craft from dropping down with the water. It is not good practice to go into a lock, going down, tie the boat up to lockside bollards and then let the water out.

The top of a weir on the River Thames. This one is provided with protection for craft that have been swept towards the weir out of control. Not all weirs are so protected but most are.

A surveyor can test the thickness of the hull using both a hammer and an ultrasound machine. Where thinning of the plate is occurring they will recommend replacement or overplating; where necessary, they will also investigate why the thinning is occurring.

FIRE

Fire can be a major disaster, as in serious cases it will completely destroy the inside of a craft and buckle the plates of the hull. While no boat is beyond repair, your insurers will consider her to be a 'total constructive loss' if the cost of reinstating the craft back to her original condition will far exceed the sum insured.

Causes and Prevention

There are many potential causes of fire on a boat. Happily, the introduction of the Certificate of Compliance in 1978, renamed the Boat Safety Scheme in 1991, has reduced many of the hazards on board, and now that the BSS is compulsory the effects have taken hold.

Some possible causes of fires are as follows:

- If the wires on your low-voltage DC system are too thin, they can overheat and start a fire.
- Candles can cause problems. Yes, they are nice to look at and save the battery, but do make sure that, if used, they cannot fall over or set fire to surrounding curtains or other boat fittings, and never leave them unattended. This might sound

A serious fire on a boat is the biggest disaster that can befall it. The inside is destroyed and smells of burning until what is left of the hull is thoroughly cleaned, and in the worst situations the plates of the hull could be buckled. While a craft can be rebuilt, most insurers will treat a bad fire as a 'constructive total loss' as the cost of reinstatement will often be greater than the sum insured under the policy.

obvious but many fires over the years have been caused by candles falling over or setting fire to furnishings. The same applies to oil lamps.
- Solid fuel stoves, if fitted properly, are perfectly safe. Hot or burning coal can fall out onto the carpet, however, so do not leave the door open. If the fire overheats, it can set fire to surrounding woodwork or clothes left to dry hanging close to the unit.
- Curtains can be blown by the wind or other causes onto the flame of the gas cooker burner if they are not properly secured.
- Mobile heaters (which are not allowed, in any case) can move and set fire to the surrounding furnishings.
- Cigarette butts and ash can be hazards if left lying around. Before going to bed, empty the ashtray somewhere safe, such as into the fire.

The above examples are all drawn from fire claims I have dealt with over the past forty years that resulted in the loss of the craft, and all could have been avoided. Be aware of the possible causes of fire and take suitable preventative measures. Finally, fit a smoke alarm – most fires start when the boat is in use.

CARBON MONOXIDE POISONING

Part of the Boat Safety Scheme certificate is to inspect both the low-level and high-level ventilation. This is to ensure that levels of carbon monoxide (CO) and carbon dioxide (CO_2) are not able to build up. Too many deaths have been caused over the years because this simple measure has been ignored by the boat owner/user.

Causes
The main cause of CO being present in the atmosphere inside your boat is a leak from an appliance such as a water heater, fridge or fire, combined with inadequate ventilation.

Prevention
Your BSS examiner or surveyor will be able to gauge if your fixed ventilation is adequate for the size of your boat – they will consider both the lower and upper ventilation, as these together enable air to circulate within the craft.

Such ventilation should always be fixed in the open position, so windows do not count, nor do mushroom vents, which can also be closed.

You could also consider fitting a CO alarm (*see* Chapter 9).

Mushroom vents are used as outlets for water heaters and also to provide high-level ventilation in a boat.

Low-level ventilation can be provided by grilles such as this in doors.

The BSS for a private pleasure craft can be issued with inadequate ventilation, providing a note is made of the lack of either high- or low-level (or both); in this case, you should take steps to remedy the situation for your own safety and that of any friends you invite onto your boat.

INJURY TO CREW

Happily such events are rare but they can happen. Very often injury is caused by the carelessness of the injured person.

Causes

If you are sitting on top of the boat or climbing up onto the roof, it might seem obvious that you need to check whether the craft is about to go under a bridge, yet people do forget, with sometimes painful consequences.

Leaving a windlass handle on the paddle gear is not a good idea. If a boat bumps into the gate the paddle can drop with the vibration and the windlass handle will fly off. At best you lose it in the canal, at worst it can hit someone at high speed and cause a nasty injury.

If someone falls in, do take the engine out of gear if they come close to the back of the boat. A person in the water could suffer injury if they come into contact with a propeller.

Lock sides can be dangerous places. Be aware of where you will end up when opening a gate. Most locks are in open country but some are a bit more compact, with little, if any, space to get around the balance beams. Getting crushed between a balance beam and a wall is not to be recommended. I also know of a man who fell off a lock wall once and down about 8ft (2.5m) onto broken glass.

Prevention

Your friends have joined you for a pleasant day out so starting the day with a lecture about safety may put a dampener on the proceedings, but you can do this without sounding like the cabin crew before take-off.

The main thing to mention is, as you hand over a windlass for the first time, that they should never leave it on the spindle.

Otherwise, just be aware of your surroundings and keep an eye on what your friends (and others) are up to.

Another good point is not to drink too much whilst boating – save that for when you are tied up!

One thing you should never do is leave the windlass handle on the paddle gear – over the years, I have seen some very nasty accidents caused by flying handles.

CHAPTER 13

RESPONSIBLE BOATING

Remember that you are sharing the waterway system with others, so do not spoil their enjoyment of boating by unthinking behaviour. Do not be a canal cowboy!

While your craft is under way it is not advisable to have too much alcohol – accidents can happen and drinking too much will reduce your ability to handle the situation, just like when driving a car.

There are a number of don'ts which many boat handlers do – and this is not just hire boaters but private boat owners as well.

SPEEDING

The first one is to *slow* down past moored craft. There are two very good reasons for this rule.

If you pass craft at too high a speed then you can pull a craft tied up alongside, in the worst-case scenario, completely off their mooring. I came back to my boat once to find my mooring chain had been snapped and some kind person had reconnected both parts with several strands of wire. Such drag can also cause damage to the infrastructure of the waterway, which is not so obvious but can build up over a long period.

MOORING UP

Also, if you are on a shallow waterway, winding your engine up will pull the back of the boat down, which will not make you go any faster but will use more fuel and distribute silt through the water.

As mentioned above, do not run your engine or a generator where the noise will affect either other boat owners moored close to you or those in buildings near by. The sound is amplified by the water surface so what may sound acceptable to you will be much worse on the other side of the waterway.

There are three ways to tie up. The first is to use bollards, which are normally provided at lock landings or such places as water points. These are not designed for long-term mooring but for temporary mooring while operating a lock or using the facilities.

Mooring rings are often provided at pubs and other locations (including visitor moorings) for craft to tie up to.

The third method is 'do it yourself', and here you have a number of options. The original and traditional method is to insert mooring pins into the towpath to which the craft can be tied. Too many boats fail to slow down when passing moored craft, however, so this is not an ideal way of tying your boat up if you are leaving it! Much of the canal system these days has piling or 'campshedding' along the bank, where the interlocking piles are driven into the bank and connected at the top with a bolted rail. The W profile of the piles creates a useful gap that can be used to tie up to. It's not a good idea to use rope for this though, as it can be cut through by the metal of the bar used to tie round; there are devices that can sit in the gap (although these can come out) or, better still, you can use a short chain with rings at either end, one of which will pass through the other. You can tie your rope to the smaller ring. This is the best method of long-term mooring away from your home mooring.

RESPONSIBLE BOATING

Bollards are sited at locks and at places such as water points to enable craft to be tied up easily. At mooring locations it is normal to provide metal rings rather than bollards.

Do not moor up at water points (except, of course, when taking on water!), on lock landings or anywhere else where your boat could cause an obstruction. Stopping too close to a bridge hole or on a bend are two examples.

When mooring up at a popular spot, do not take a space slap bang in the middle between two other craft but moor close to one or the other, thus leaving room for another craft to moor. Do not get your generator out either – other boaters have come out to enjoy the peace and tranquillity of the waterways, not to listen to your generator!

Remember when mooring up that your ropes should not pass across the towpath and you should only tie to your own mooring equipment (such as mooring pins) and not to such things as scaffolding or water point equipment, no matter how convenient they may look.

Another point is not to moor up using a centre line. This should only be used to pull the boat in and as a temporary measure while securing ropes fore and aft.

USING ROPES

As mentioned earlier, there are three basic types of line used on a narrow boat:

A **long line**, or snubber, is seldom used these days but having one in the engine room is always a good

The chain is passed through the longitudinal support strip connecting the piles inserted into the canal bank for bank protection. There is a small ring at one end which passes through a larger ring at the other end of the chain. A rope from the boat is then passed through the smaller ring and tied to the dolly on the deck of the boat. This is a quick and efficient way of tying a boat up on about half the canal system.

idea. These are normally about 70ft (21m) long and are used to tow a butty on long pounds, which makes it easier for both craft to get along.

Cross straps are seldom used by single craft but are used by a pair of craft to tow the butty hard up against the stern of the motor.

Straps, the normal line used on narrow boats and other craft in modern times, are about 30ft in length. They are used as throwing lines, mooring ropes and for all sorts of other things. In my experience, a single eye splice at one end and nothing at the other is most practical, but this is personal preference. One or two of these should be kept at the bow of the boat and a couple at the stern.

Today ropes are often made of nylon but you can still obtain cotton line, sisal and other types.

Never hang your strap on the tiller pin. Some folk think this is traditional but it is not and in fact is dangerous for a number of reasons. At best you can pull your tiller pin out (should this happen, a screwdriver will do in its place!) or worse, get it caught around the prop. At best this will stall your engine and take ages to unravel, while at worst you could cause damage to the engine and associated parts.

It is also not a good idea to keep rope on the back deck, as this could also end up round the prop and, in addition, causes a trip hazard. The best place is on the cabin top, coiled ready for use. Here they are in line of sight, and it is far easier to grab a rope you can see while still controlling your boat. When

94 RESPONSIBLE BOATING

required, slip the eye over the dolly or bollard on the stern.

For those who say it is easier to hang a rope on the tiller pin, it may well seem so but the risks outweigh the convenience. It also hides your pin, which, with the modern trend to have some quite fancy units on display, would defeat the object!

When you tie up you should take care to pass the rope from your boat to a fixed point on the edge of the waterway. Your rope should not cross the towpath, as this would be a trip hazard to other towpath users.

WORKING LOCKS

It is quite possible for one person to work a boat through a lock – it is just hard work! On a narrow canal you are better off with two people and on a wide canal three – after the boat is in and going up or down, the third person can head off to set the

A Grand Union lock showing the gates, lock gear and bollards found at all locks, regardless of size.

BELOW: *These gate paddles on the bottom gates of a lock enable the user to wind up two paddles at the same time. Ground paddles only have one.*

Until the early 1990s, the steerer of a craft working down a lock had to guess where the cill was. From that date the then British Waterways Board started painting white lines on the side, providing some much-needed guidance.

next lock, unless it is already in use, ready for the boat to arrive. The more people you have, the easier it is!

Always check the paddles at the other end of the lock: while the crew of the last boat to use the lock should have ensured that the paddles are fully down, they may not be. If the paddles are not down all the way, water will still pass through the sluice, which you may not notice until you realize that your boat is taking a long time to reach the correct level.

Be aware of hazards such as getting the boat caught on the cill or getting hung up (*see* Chapter 11).

If the lock is against you (that is, you are going up and the lock is full or you are working down and it is empty), do check to make sure that there is not a boat coming towards you from the other direction. If there is, wait for them to use the lock and then you can use it in turn. This avoids wasting water and upsetting those in the boat coming the other way who will have to wait much longer to use the lock while you set it for your boat and then use it.

The basic way of working a single lock is the same going uphill or down. Going down you have to be aware of the cill, and going up you have to make sure you do not catch the nose of the boat in the lock gate!

Approach the lock, and either drop off crew or get off yourself if single-handed, to tie the boat up, perhaps on a centre line (a rope connected to a point on the centre of the boat and running back down the roof to the steering position).

If the lock is in your favour, open the gate and return to your boat to take it into the lock.

If the lock is against you, check to make sure that there is not a boat heading towards you – if there is then they should use the lock first. If there is no boat in sight then close the gate or gates, check that the paddles are down and return to your end of the lock and fill or empty the lock in favour of your boat.

Once your boat is in the lock, make sure no paddles have been left up by the previous user and then raise the paddles to let water in (if going up) or out (if going down), remembering to keep an eye out to make sure that your boat does not get caught on the cill going down or in the gate going up. It's been said before but is worth repeating!

If you are in a lock you need to be alert at all times. A friend of mine, while working uphill, set the paddles and then promptly went off to empty his loo. When he came back he discovered his boat had lifted off the lock gate! He was very embarrassed.

When operating the paddles, do not 'whip 'em up' but take the paddle up one third at a time. This will reduce the water flow, which in a narrow lock can shoot the boat backwards and forwards and in a wide lock throws the boat from side to side. The best way is to raise the paddles a third at a time and allow the water flow to settle before the next third. This only applies to a lock with a boat in – if the lock is empty, the paddles can be raised as fast as the operator can manage.

Once the level is made, you can open the gate and take the boat out.

Do lower the paddles and check that they are fully down.

There are different rules for how you leave a lock. If in doubt, close the gates. Some locks require you to leave the lock with the lock full. Some have to be empty, some with the gates open but the paddles down. Be aware that there are many notices on lock gates instructing you how to leave a lock – only act on an official notice, though, as for some reason there are many unofficial notices being placed on locks.

SOUND SIGNALS

It is surprising how few boat owners know about the existence of sound signals.

One long blast is a warning indicator that can be used as you are approaching a blind bend or bridge to warn any boater coming towards you of your presence.

The warning blast can be used on its own or in conjunction with other signals, as follows:

One short blast – 'I am turning right or passing you on my left'

RESPONSIBLE BOATING

Two short blasts – 'I am turning left or passing you on my right'
Three short blasts – 'My engine is in reverse'
Four short blasts – 'I am unable to manoeuvre'
Five short blasts – 'I do not consider that you are taking sufficient action to avoid a collision'

The above were the signals recommended by the then British Waterways Board. There are some other sound signals listed by the Canal and River Trust but the ones given here are the main ones in use by those who know of their existence!

If you are approaching a bridge and a boat is coming the other way, the boat furthest from the bridge should slow down to allow the other boat priority. The exception to this is a pair with the motor towing a butty – let them through even if you are closer to the bridge.

The second most popular leisure activity on the inland waterways, after boating, is angling. The towpath is also used by many other people, such as walkers and cyclists.

There are so many canalside pubs it is hard to choose just one to illustrate! The Boat Inn, opposite the Canal Museum in Stoke Bruerne, has been part of my association with canals since the 1960s and is now being run by the sixth generation of the same family.

RESPONSIBLE BOATING

If you are approaching a sharp bend or a blind bridge then assume that there is a boat coming the other way and slow down. Let any possible craft know you are there with one long blast on your horn.

OTHER WATERWAY USERS

The canal system was built for the passage of craft carrying goods but this use is now, in the main, in the past. In the same way, the towpath, or towing path, was used by horses to tow such boats. This is now even less common. You are unlikely these days to see a heavy horse towing a boat, although there is a Horse Boat Society who have craft that are still moved in this way.

The working boats have been largely replaced by pleasure craft, but there are also other groups of people who use the waterways for work or leisure, who are also entitled to be treated with consideration.

The most numerous of these is the angler. Most will respond to a cheery hello, but there are some, as in all walks of life, who either ignore the passing boater or who can even be rude. These are, happily, the minority. The best thing to do when boating past anglers is to carry on as if they were not there – in other words, keep to the centre of the cut and stay at 4mph (6km/h). Do not slow down – they want you past as soon as possible – but do not speed up either. The last thing you should do is pull over to the far side of the waterway, which is where the 'swims' are. That is why anglers have such long poles.

Difficulties do occur. What do you do when you come to a long line of moored craft with just one space you can fit into but that is being used by

The heron is, perhaps, the symbol of these peaceful waterways, which are home to a great diversity of wildlife.

anglers? Frankly, you simply have to explain that this is the only spot where you can tie up, but do it in a polite and friendly way. Most anglers will understand.

Finding anglers fishing from opposite a winding hole or even by or in a lock (as I did once), despite the 'no fishing' signs, will often produce a heated debate. Try to keep calm and explain the problem. A heated debate is often something no one wins and will spoil the day for both sides. Do not lose your temper – no one else wants it!

Towpaths are also often used by walkers and cyclists. Walkers rarely present a problem to the boater, and most cyclists travel at a slow speed dictated by the condition of the path. In some areas the surface of the towpath is flat and smooth, surfaced with either tarmac or concrete. Here the speeding cyclist may be encountered. Many verbal clashes have occurred between speeding cyclists and other users of the system.

There are areas where the towpath has been dug up to bury all sorts of services, such as fibre-optic cables, gas pipelines and power cables; I know one stretch of towpath where there are no fewer than five linear services buried beneath.

It was the railways who first discovered that the route they had taken could also be used for telegraph cables. The idea was quickly taken up, and today canals, railways and motorways provide an easy route from one part of the country to another for all sorts of such services.

Wildlife also use canals as a linear corridor, and as you cruise along you will see all types of birds and, if you look closely, mammals scurrying along the banks. This must rank as one of the great attractions of boating.

CHAPTER 14

GOING FURTHER

ORGANIZATIONS AND NAVIGATION AUTHORITIES

In these days of the internet, there is little point in providing a list of telephone numbers and addresses. For example, in the last five years or so, the Inland Waterways Association has moved from Rickmansworth to Chesham, and the British Waterways Board has been replaced in England and Wales by the Canal and River Trust and the offices are now in Milton Keynes not Watford. It's quicker and more reliable for the reader to look up contact information online for the organizations mentioned in this book.

MUSEUMS

There are a number of museums around the canal system reflecting life in the days of carrying. The

There are three national waterways museums and dozens of local museums on the inland network. This is Llanthony warehouse in Gloucester Docks, which is the home of the largest museum operated by the Canal and River Trust.

GOING FURTHER

three main ones are at Gloucester Docks, Stoke Bruerne and Ellesmere Port; these are run by the Canal and River Trust. There are also others of varying size dotted about the country run by local trusts or organizations such as the London Canal Museum in Kings Cross. All provide an interesting visit.

Many such organizations own or operate ex-working craft kept in traditional condition, and some offer trips on the canal as well as or as part of an educational visit. While a number of these craft can only be viewed externally, others have been restored internally as well and visitors can go inside (which is not to say that craft not open for inspection haven't been restored internally, of course!). Others are used as visitor centres, cafés, exhibition displays and similar purposes.

GAINING EXPERIENCE

If you are new to boating and want to gain some knowledge and experience before you buy your boat, there are a number of boat-handling courses available to teach you the basics.

Another way to gain experience is to hire a boat. You will be (or should be) given a short instruction session, if required, prior to leaving the base, and this should include such things as how to work locks as well as the operation of the craft and its engine.

If the hire company is a member of British Marine they will provide you with a set handover course before you take the boat away.

JOINING A GROUP

Elsewhere in this book I have mentioned volunteer groups you can join. I recommend this as it is a good way to meet like-minded enthusiasts.

The Inland Waterways Association is perhaps your first choice. With the many branches it has across the country, you will never be far from a monthly meeting where you can meet other boaters and perhaps become involved in the waterways movement.

The other organizations I have mentioned will be worth joining depending on your specific interest.

In winter months a hire boat base has all or most of the craft to be hired out on the base wharf.

GOING FURTHER

Many hold boat gatherings or rallies that you may wish to attend.

Finally, you can also find groups online on such platforms as Facebook and Twitter. There are a number of Facebook groups, for example, that provide the opportunity for those new to boating to ask questions or seek assistance from others – a very useful system.

RIVER BOATING

Narrow boats were designed to travel on the smooth waters of the canal and not to cope with the flow of water to be found on a river. Many inland non-tidal rivers are quite safe, but you should remember that levels can change overnight (OK, they can do that on the canal too if someone leaves a paddle up!), that the banks are often private property and there may not be a towpath.

You should always carry an anchor with chain and rope connected to the upstream end of the craft.

Keep well away from weirs, and if river staff advise you to tie up in strong stream conditions – do so!

Tidal rivers can be a greater hazard. You not only have the fact that the water levels change twice a day but the downstream current may be stronger than your engine can cope with – and this situation can change very quickly. It is always a good idea to travel in pairs (the buddy boat system) so that, in the event of a problem, one boat can come to the assistance of the other.

A VHF radio is also a good idea and, on some waterways, is a requirement. You need a licence to operate such a device but the course and exam are fairly simple.

Check your planned route with your insurers to make sure you will be covered, and perhaps with a local boat club, who have a better knowledge of the waterway you plan to cross than most. As an example, many narrow boats take passage on the Thames from Limehouse to Brentford or Teddington. A chat with St Pancras Cruising Club in this instance is a jolly good idea, and the IWA have a cruising guide to the Thames Tideway on their website.

OVERSEAS BOATING

Narrow boats are not designed to be taken to sea, and although a number have made it across the Channel under their own power, this is not recommended. A narrow boat can be adapted to provide a better platform but even so, the weather can change dramatically in the time it takes to make the crossing.

The Thames in central London sometimes sees narrow boats in transit from Limehouse to Brentford. Such a trip should be taken with care and ideally in company with another craft. A VHF radio is also recommended.

Narrow boats and other craft are often lifted out of the water, either for exterior hull work or for transporting by lorry to another part of the system or abroad.

The best way to take your boat abroad is to have it lifted out in the UK and taken by road and ferry to a location on the continent where it can be lifted in again.

There are specialist firms who will undertake this for you and provide both the crane and the lorry with trailer.

The waterways of the continent are vast and you can spend years of long weekends and holidays exploring the system, but you should research the project in full before you even think about booking the crane. Things to consider include items such as what licence(s) you will need and moorings (both short-term and long-term – that is, a 'home' mooring). This is the subject for a whole book in its own right – or perhaps several books!

CONCLUSION

This book scratches the surface of what is involved with owning a narrow boat and I hope you will find it a useful starting point. There are books available that go more deeply into individual subjects than the space allows in this general guide. Some books cover the entire system or go into greater detail about a particular region or individual waterway, while others deal with specific subjects such as boat painting and decoration, types of boat and maintenance. A number of publishers issue guidebooks and maps of the inland waterways system, normally on a regional basis. You can buy many of these by mail order from the Inland Waterways Association or specialist booksellers.

You can also download apps onto your phone that tell you what services and facilities are available in your area. I must be honest, I do prefer a physical guidebook that I can keep in the drawer at the back of my boat.

There are a number of monthly magazines available from your local newsagent, plus two or three free monthly newspapers available at boat clubs, boatyards and canalside pubs. Both the CRT and the IWA publish a regular newsletter available over the internet, and, of course, their websites provide you with up-to-date information regarding the waterways.

At the time of writing, there have been several recent television series produced relating to waterway topics. Some of these are better researched than others!

If you are new to the waterways I hope you have found this book a useful starting point and trust that you will get as much fun and interest out of both the history of the system and using it.

GLOSSARY

Like any group of people, inland boat owners have a private language of words and phrases that relate to the inland waterways and are different from those used by river boaters and sea-going boaters. These words are not restricted to narrow boats, although most are narrow boat terms. Most are historical but there are some more modern additions.

Some of these, together with other general terms applicable to boating, are listed below in alphabetical order.

Alarms There are a number of different alarms on the market that will be suitable for use on any boat.

The first and most important – indeed, essential – is a CO (Carbon Monoxide) alarm. Not having one on your boat could kill you and anyone else on your boat! CO is a deadly killer and, however careful you are, it is quite possible for CO to seep into the living area of your craft. The next in order of importance is a smoke alarm. This (if you keep the battery fresh) will wake you up if there is a fire on your boat during the night. Next most important is – if you have gas/LPG on your boat – a gas alarm. This will detect a gas leak should you have one. Since the introduction of BSS standards, leaks happen less often.

Finally there is the question of an intruder alarm. Some boats are fitted with such a device but these can be set off if the boat is rocked in high winds or even stepped onto by people crossing the craft. If the boat is broken into, who will hear the alarm go off? A new device is available to show up on your mobile telephone with a camera inside your boat so you can see exactly what is going on. If you are away from the boat and it is in a marina or is moored in a location where you can contact someone, you can ring them and ask if they could investigate or perhaps ring the local police.

Anchor An anchor is used on flowing water to hold the craft. It is a metal device attached to a length of chain and rope that can be thrown overboard in the event that the craft needs to be held, such as a loss of engine power. The anchor works both by its weight and its flukes (arms) digging into the bed of the waterway, and holds the craft.

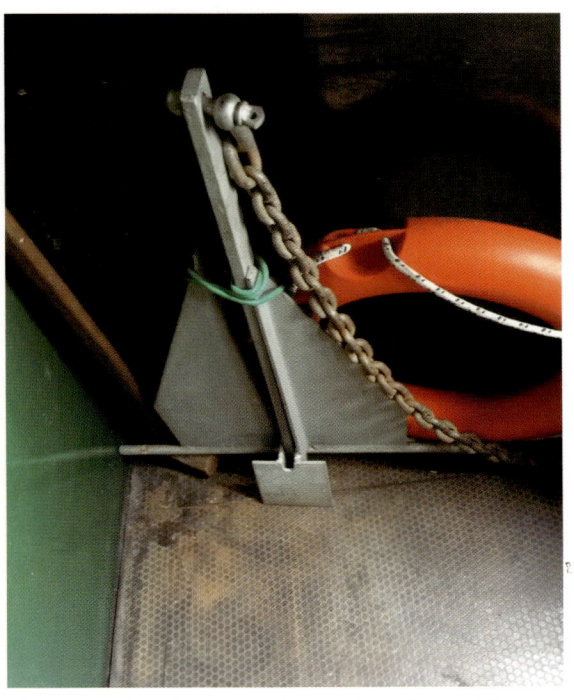

If you are planning to venture onto a river with your narrow boat you will need to carry an anchor and lifebelt.

GLOSSARY

The type of anchor and chain you need depends on the weight of your boat and, to some degree, what waterways you intend to navigate on. Your local chandlery will be pleased to advise you.

Anodes These are lumps of metal welded to the underside of the craft that are sacrificial in nature. They are often placed at the bow and stern of the craft to provide some protection against deterioration of the hull from corrosion. They are made of a metal that is more reactive to the water environment than the metal the hull is made from, so they will corrode before the hull does (hence 'sacrificial'). There are two types of anode – one for salt water and one for fresh water; these are magnesium. They should be placed 'in sight' of each other to give overall protection to the hull so you will need several.

Aqueduct Canals can be carried over rivers on bridges but a valley requires a larger structure. This is the aqueduct. There are many examples all over the system, but probably the most famous is Pontcysyllte in North Wales.

Anodes are welded to the hull to protect it from wear caused by electrolytic action. They will waste as they do their job and thus need to be replaced on a regular basis.

Anser pin A shackle in the gunwale just forward of the counter, to use when breasting up.

Most views of this famous structure show the aqueduct from the side. This shot shows the boater's view. The canal is taken across the river valley below in an iron trough. Note there is no rail on the non-towpath side.

An anser pin used to assist with 'buttying up' – tying a butty to a motor boat side by side. It can also be used when tying up.

GLOSSARY

The canal system today still has many arms off the main line, which enabled craft to get to warehouses and factories. There used to be many more, and evidence of their location can still often be found.

Anti-cavitation plate A plate to cover the bottom of the weed hatch that is flush with the uxter plate (the bottom of the counter).

Arm The main lines of the canal system went from one important point to another, but there were sections of waterway (arms) leading off these main lines to various locations that would not otherwise be connected to the system. Most of these were fairly short but some were quite long. Some of these arms still exist and are used today as boatyards or moorings but many have fallen into disuse and, in most cases, have been filled in.

BACAT Two types of craft used for carrying goods on the inland waterways that could be taken overseas on parent ships and put back onto the inland system once in port. LASH stood for Lighter Aboard Ship and BACAT stood for Barge Aboard Catamaran. LASH craft were developed in the 1960s and BACAT in the mid-70s; neither are in use now.

Back cabin The living area on a working narrow boat, just forward of the steering position. It was a cosy little room, about 8ft by 6ft (2.5m by 2m), with a stove, a larder where the door came down as a table, a single side bed that doubled as a seat during the day, and a double bed across the boat

The cramped inside of a back cabin on a motor boat with the cross bed at the back and all other equipment, such as the stove, round the side. The table cupboard comes down to form a table. The side bed is used as a seat during the day.

at the rear of the cabin. Beyond this (going forward) was the engine room on a motor boat or the hold on a butty. Painted in traditional narrow boat style with 'scumbled' paintwork, this was the home of the crew.

Backering When a horse towed the craft on its own without a handler. The horse had to be trained to do this but most took to the idea quite well.

Banbury stick A pole with a length of rope attached that was used to hold up a lift bridge and could be pulled out after the boat had passed through, allowing the bridge to fall back into place. Its use was discouraged for perhaps obvious reasons by the CRT and is not something you should try today.

Barge A barge is a vessel wider than a boat! There is no definition that gives us an exact size, but any craft over 7ft (2.1m) can be treated as a barge, including short boats, Dutch barges, keels and modern craft that have been built for use on the inland waterways. The basic difference is that, as the craft are larger, the premiums are higher and the cruising range is wider.

Blue top A number of narrow boats were fitted with GRP covers or hoops that could be used instead of sheets of tarpaulin to cover the hold. In

A barge converted from cargo carrying to residential use. Many ex-working craft, both narrow boats and barges, have been so converted.

This boat, with an extended cabin, has been fitted with blue tops to cover a living area, which makes the craft look as though it is still in working trim.

GLOSSARY

Bollards are used for quick and easy temporary mooring. They can be found at locks and at other key waterside locations.

with a hull inspection. BSS examiners are not surveyors and are not insured to examine the hull of a boat. A surveyor, if requested and if registered with BSS, can issue a BSS certificate alongside a hull inspection. Not all navigation authorities require BSS certifications, but the main two, the Canal and River Trust and the Environment Agency, do.

Bollards Short, sturdy posts set into the ground at locks, water points and similar locations for craft to tie up to temporarily. *See also* Rings, Pins.

Bow hauling A way of hauling a butty through narrow locks where the motor had already passed through. The line was not attached to the bow, as the term suggests, but back through to runners to the mast, just over a quarter of the way back from the bow.

the main, these were the River-class and Admiralty-class boats built in the 1950s. The covers could be stacked up during unloading. As they were blue in colour the name 'blue top' was given to the covers and the craft, and the term is still used today. While very few are still used on commercial carrying craft, the plastic covers can still be found all over the canal system serving a number of purposes, including providing a 'lid' or superstructure to ex-working craft.

Boat Safety Scheme The boat equivalent of an MOT, designed to improved safety on the waterways. The Certificate of Compliance was launched by the British Waterways Board (BWB) in 1978 and was replaced by the BSS in 1991. It became compulsory in 1997. A BSS certificate should never be accepted in lieu of a survey but can be accepted

Bow thruster Tube fitted across the craft at the bow with a propeller inside it. Operated by remote control from the steering position, it is used to help push the bow round when turning, or pushing the front of the boat away from the bank. However, it is often used by the inexperienced in the wrong situation and is not an essential piece of equipment.

Breach Because the canal needs to keep level between locks there are times when the waterway will be under (in a cutting or tunnel) the level of the surrounding land or above it (on an embankment or aqueduct). Due to subsidence, bad weather or another reason, the bank can give way, causing a breach. This results in loss of water from the canal, local flooding and possible damage to craft moored near the breach.

GLOSSARY 111

A repaired length of canal following a breach. A sudden breach of a canal can cause a number of problems, including flooding to surrounding land and property and leaving craft in the section on the bottom. Not only are craft prevented from using the route until the breach can be repaired, but it is an urgent and additional cost to the navigation authority.

In March 2018, a serious breach closed the Middlewich branch of the Shropshire Union Canal. Here you can see the breach itself and the boats stranded as a result.

GLOSSARY

Breasted pair leaving a lock. Sadly they have not lowered the paddle or closed the gates. It is traditional on the Grand Union to leave one gate open (for a number of very good reasons) but the paddles should be lowered.

Breasted up A term to describe two boats moored or travelling tied to each other side by side, as was normal in short pounds with a motor and butty. The term can also apply to two motor boats. The two boats so joined could be handled as one craft 14ft (4.2m) wide, which meant that there was no need for a steerer on the butty boat.

Bridges A way of crossing over a waterway. There are many bridges over the inland waterways, carrying both road and rail traffic. On the canal system the majority are fairly standard and cause a narrowing of the canal to make building the bridge less expensive.

There are many odd-shaped bridges on our inland waterways system. This example shows a road bridge with the canal in a deep cutting. The middle section supports a telegraph pole.

GLOSSARY 113

We are used to the basic canal bridges that can be found all over the canal network, but sometimes we come across more ornate specimens. These were normally built at the insistence of a local landowner as part of the agreement to allow the canal to pass through his land.

Bridge guard An iron or steel plate on the towpath side of a bridge, designed to protect brickwork from damage caused by the rubbing of tow ropes. In these plates you can see the grooves dug by the friction of a rope as the horse went under the bridge. Despite the fact that it is over a hundred years since motors were introduced onto the canals, you can still find these guards in place on the bridges.

The iron plate was fixed to the bridge to stop tow ropes cutting into the brickwork and thus damaging the bridge. You can clearly see the grooves cut by the ropes.

Here you can see how the rope connecting the horse and the boat would rub away at the structure of the bridge where the tow rope cut into the iron.

Bridge guards also describe a pair of beams that start at the bow of a boat and extend to the fore end of the cabin. These guide boats into bridge holes on narrow canals and help to guard against damage to the cabin superstructure. They were found mainly on hire boats but were also installed on some private pleasure craft, but do present a trip hazard when climbing on or off the fore end of a craft.

Bridge hole Where the canal narrows underneath a bridge. On the canals, bridges were built to allow roads to pass over the waterway. The most common type of bridge is of a hump-back design and the distance from one side of the bridge to the other was the same as a lock on the waterway plus room for the towpath. This was done to keep the cost down. As boats cannot pass at such locations, one boat has to 'hold back' to allow the other through. The bridge was constructed using wooden arches placed over the canal and, on the Southern Stratford, cottages can be found made of these wooden arches once they had served their original purpose – an early form of recycling!

Buckby can A can used on working craft to carry water for cooking, washing and drinking. It looks a bit like an upside-down bucket with a handle and a spout. As with most things on narrow boats, the cans are painted with flowers and castles and often have the name of the boat painted on the front. They are understood to have first been made in Long Buckby, a canal village on the Grand Union in Northamptonshire, hence the name.

The standard type of bridge found on the canal system all over the country. The canal was narrowed to reduce the cost of the bridge, and the resulting gap is the 'bridge hole'.

GLOSSARY   115

A Buckby can was used to carry water on commercial craft that were not fitted with water tanks. They were filled up from taps located at locks.

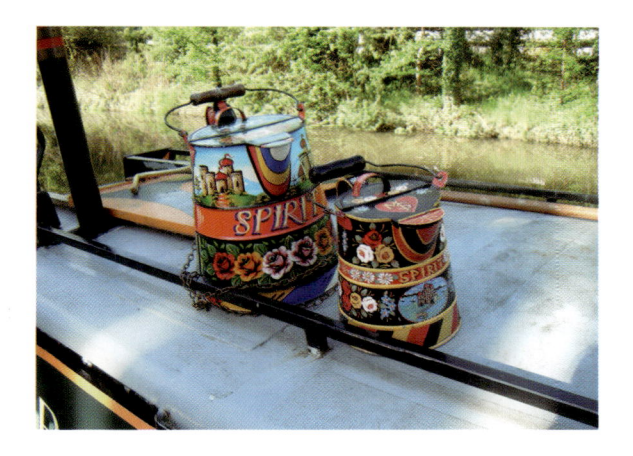

Budget   A fixed rudder on a lighter essential for steering when being towed by a tug or other craft.

Bulkhead   A wall inside a boat that can be structural or cosmetic. Narrow boats were not originally built with watertight bulkheads between the engine room and the rest of the hold, although some modern craft are. Most narrow boats sink due to ingress of water at the rear of the craft, so fitting a watertight bulkhead between the stern area and the rest of the craft will prevent the craft from sinking and reduce the claim cost from thousands to hundreds. Regrettably, there is no legal requirement for this simple safety device, but so many craft are not fitted in this way that the cost of implementing such a requirement would be a great burden on the bulk of boat owners.

Butane   A type of liquid petroleum gas that is supplied from the cylinder (often blue) at a lower pressure than propane and has a higher calorific value. It is not liked by boat owners as it is affected by cold weather.

Butty   An unpowered narrow boat designed to be towed by a motor (narrow boat). It was for this reason that the Grand Union was 'doubled' (the locks were made wider) – so that a motor and butty could work through the lock side by side. Horse boats would often work in pairs for the same reason – it made working through a wide lock easier.

This shot shows a butty from the rear while being towed. You can see the butty tiller in the under-way position and the size of the rudder needed to bite into the water flow. This is a hotel pair and you can see that the cabin over the hold is much higher than the original back cabin.

The original craft were ex-horse boats but in the 1920s/30s, large fleets of pairs of boats were built with butty boats designed to run with motors. Both horse boats and butties had much larger rudders and a beam tiller that slotted into the top of the rudder post. Some butties are moved by an outboard motor strapped either to the side of the craft or to the rudder, but neither is a really effective method of moving the boat about. A 'motor butty' – a butty which has been motorized with an inboard engine – can be regarded as a conversion to a motor boat.

Buttying up Putting two boats side by side (breasting up) or towing.

A breasted pair of Grand Union boats. You can see the masts with the top planks in the lower position.

BELOW: *Another pair, this time an FMC one.*

GLOSSARY

Campshedding Piles or boards lining the riverbank to prevent erosion.

Cants Upside-down L-shaped metal strips at the join of the upper hull and the decking, originally used on wooden craft to protect the bow and stern from damage. Not required on modern steel craft, they are still built in today out of tradition.

Caulking Sealing the gaps between planks on a wooden craft to keep it watertight. The material used for this, rolled oakum (hemp fibre), is inserted carefully between the planks using special hammers and a caulking iron.

Centre line A line from the mast or a point on the roof of a modern narrow boat for temporary mooring, for example while waiting at a lock.

Chaining in On working craft, there was no superstructure to hold in the sides of a narrow boat and thus the craft can 'spread', resulting, in some cases, in the craft getting stuck in a lock. This was solved by attaching chains to special points in the hold, just under the gunwale, which were tightened by windlass to hold the sides in. Chains are also used when tying up a boat for a long period. There is less chance of a craft being turned loose from its mooring if you can attach a chain to the campshedding (piling) or some other fixed point.

Chine Where the bottom of the craft meets the side. On a narrow boat, the bottom plate sticks out to protect the weld from damage by running along the bottom of the canal, hence the term 'sacrificial chine'. As this is the section of the craft most liable to external damage, this is something that needs to be monitored carefully in a survey. Wear to the chine can eventually result in water flowing into the craft. The chine should be welded both inside and out, although this is not often done by modern boatyards.

The chine is where the bottom or base of a craft meets the side. To prevent wear, which could result in holes in the craft sinking the boat, the bottom edge protrudes about ½in (1cm). Every so often this will need to be repaired.

A chain taken round the connecting strip of the piling or campshedding and used to tie the boat up – a sort of instant mooring ring.

Cill A shelf at the top end of a lock that sticks out 1–3ft (30–90cm) from the bottom gates and is level with the bottom of the canal at the higher level above the lock. It is possible, if working down a lock, for the boat to drift back and to catch the stern on the cill. This can cause damage to the rudder and other parts of the rear of the craft. In the worst situation, in a deep lock, the craft can sink or turn over.

Cloths Tarpaulins that protect the hold cargo on a working boat. Side cloths go from the gunwale upwards, while top cloths drape over the top planks that run down the boat resting on the mast and stands. The side cloths go under the top cloths so that water can run off into the canal. These days there are only a few hundred craft that are still 'open' and can be fitted with cloths. Many ex-working boats have been converted in a way that makes it look as though the craft is still in working trim and under canvas, but really there is a hard wood or steel superstructure under the sheets.

The cill is the bottom of the canal at the higher level and can damage the back of the boat or even sink it if the unwary steerer lets the boat get too near the top gate.

The nearer of these two boats is 'clothed up' with tarpaulins tied to the gunwale and supported over the top planks. This system was used to provide some protection for cargo in bad weather.

GLOSSARY 119

Commercial craft Boats used for business purposes. Commercial use can take many forms on the inland waterways but perhaps the most important is maintenance of the system by the navigation authorities. In many cases craft used for this have been converted from carrying craft although most these days are purpose-built. The most common commercial boats are 'work flats', which are punt-shaped with one or two small cabins and an open area for materials. These are either moved into place by a tug or can be powered by an outboard motor.

There are many maintenance craft on the inland waterways and some of them are purpose-designed dredgers. The craft uses a hydraulic bucket to raise silt from the bed of the canal and put it into a lighter alongside – a long and arduous task.

BELOW: *A tug, a lighter and a work flat in BWB green. A work flat is a sort of mobile workshop that can be moved around the system either by a tug or with an outboard motor. This example has two cabins.*

Composite craft A narrow boat built with iron sides and an elm bottom. Later steel was used and there are some boats with steel bottoms and iron sides and others with elm bottoms and steel sides.

Contour canal A canal that follows the contour line of the land. Early canals were longer than they needed to be as the cut was taken around hills on the same level to avoid the need for expensive earthworks, tunnels and locks. While this kept the cost of building down, it increased the length of time it took to get from A to B. This was not a problem in the early days as the canals had no competition. Later canals took a more direct route, which involved more work in construction, and thus more cost, but meant that goods could reach their destination much more quickly. Hugging the contour of a hill means not only a longer journey but also many more curves in the track of the waterway, which in turn restricts (or should restrict) the speed of the craft.

Counter On a narrow boat, the counter is the base of the boat above the swim (see Swim) as it tapers towards the propeller. The craft should be ballasted so that the counter is just under the normal waterline when not under way.

Craft sides Facing the front of the craft, the right-hand side is called the starboard side, from 'steer board', which was like a rudder but was on the right-hand side of the craft. To avoid damage to the steer board the craft always tied up on the left-hand side when in port so this was called the port side. Craft pass each other port to port, again to avoid damage to the steer board. The bottom foot or so of the craft sides (on a narrow boat) are called the footings.

Cratch A cratch, or deck board, is the vertical triangular-shaped board at the front of a narrow boat. It was designed to tie the cloths to and to support the top plank, which ran along the hold supported by the box masts. Originally, what is now called the cratch was the board that sat on the

The counter stern of Spirit *just after being grit blasted and having two-coat epoxy applied.*

cratch, which was the front deck, and the triangular board was called the deck board. This sat on the cratch, or front of the boat. These days, however, the word cratch is used to refer to the deck board. The cratch board is not only decorative but can also keep water out of the craft if a lock weirs (excess water flows over the top of the gates).

Cross straps See Rope.

Cross winding When a 6ft 10in (2.08m) beam boat enters a 7ft (2.1m) wide lock at a slight angle, rather than dead on the forward motion of the craft causes dents in the hull. Under normal conditions these dents are cosmetic and do not cause structural damage to the craft, but in the worst cases, a weld can split or a plate can be ruptured. Such damage is, happily, rare.

Cut Another word for a canal. A canal was cut through the landscape by navigators (navvies). It is

The deck board on this boat, which has been converted to private pleasure or residential use, is undecorated. It shows the outline of the tumblehome (profile) of the cloths or tarpaulins, which would be draped over the hull from the top planks.

Spirit *on the Shropshire Union: a narrow canal in a cutting.*

a term still used today to describe the canal among canal enthusiasts.

Cutlass bearing The bearing where the propeller shaft leaves the hull.

Cutter Where the exhaust of an engine goes out through the roof of the boat the escaping gases are taken up through a chimney. At the top of this is a circular strip of (normally) brass called a cutter. It diverts the gas and stops it from blasting bits off the tunnel roofs all over the top of the back cabin and anyone on the stern.

Diesel bug Modern diesel has an element of biodiesel in it and this can cause a small 'bug' to thrive in the fuel tank, which can clog the fuel filters. After filling with diesel, a shot of 'antidote' should be mixed in with the fuel.

Double or paired locks Two locks side by side to aid traffic flow, such as on the Regent's Canal in London (now only one lock in use) and at Hillmorton on the North Oxford. The term is sometimes wrongly used to describe a wide lock.

Draught The underwater depth of the craft, that is from the bottom of the craft to the waterline. If someone asks you how much you draw they are asking how deep you boat is in the water not how much you earn (a conversation I heard once!). The draught will be greater at the stern because of the weight of the engine. If you run aground (see Stem up) the best way out is to reverse slowly while rocking the craft.

Dutch barges A barge built in the Netherlands. There are a number of both Dutch (and French) craft on the inland waterways of the UK. For insurance purposes they are treated like any other inland barge. The most common types are Tjalks and Aaks but there are others. Very often the name of the town of build precedes the type name.

This Tjalk was originally built for maintenance work. Brought to England, it was converted to a houseboat in the late 1960s.

Electrolysis Decomposition of a steel hull by electric current, often caused by an earth leak in the 12v system or by being plugged into a mains supply not fitted with an RDC.

Ellum Canal term for helm (tiller and rudder arrangement).

Employment The waterway system can provide employment in a number of ways. There is the maintenance work undertaken by navigation authorities directly or by contractors on their behalf. Then there are opportunities for boat repair workers and boat builders, those operating hire fleets and boatyards and staff working on the many trip and restaurant boats, not to mention those who operate carrying craft and floating shops, most of whom are self-employed. In addition, there are many businesses based on or near a waterway that rely on the trade brought to them by the waterway and those using the system.

All along the waterways you will find small businesses, such as boatyards, serving the waterways. In the main these use old canal buildings but some are purpose-built.

GLOSSARY

Engine room/engine hole The engine room or hole was forward of the back cabin on a narrow boat, and the shaft ran under the back cabin to the rear of the boat. It contained the engine and fuel tank and was used for storage of tools and other items that could not be kept in the back cabin. On modern boats the engine is normally (but not always) at the stern.

Feeder (or leat) A small watercourse used to feed water to a mill or navigation. These are not normally navigable but some (such as from Trevor to Horse Shoe Falls) can be navigated with care.

The entrance to the feeder from the River Dee into the Shropshire Union canal at Trevor. The feeder is accessible to craft almost to the point where the Dee feeds the canal.

On an ex-working craft the engine room will be forward of the back cabin, but many modern craft with a traditional stern have the engine room at the stern. Semi-trad and cruiser-stern craft have the engine under the back deck.

GLOSSARY 125

Fenders Bumpers that are fitted to the front and stern of a craft to protect the hull (and anything the craft may hit!). The one at the stern of a narrow boat is called a button, and the one at the front a tipcat, although both can be used in either position. Fitting of fenders fore and aft is required by the CRT. There are also side fenders, which are hung on the side of the craft.

Flat A maintenance or work boat on a canal. Normally 35ft by 6ft 10in (10.7m by 2m) beam, they are either unpowered or have outboards fitted. They are punt shaped and often have little huts or cabins at one end. In the main they were built for the BWB, mostly in the 1960s, but some have transferred to private companies, who use them as work boats, and some have been converted for private pleasure use. 'Flat' is also the name given to larger craft that used to work on the rivers Mersey and Weaver. Although they were not built to a standard size, the bulk of them were 65ft by 16ft (19.8m by 4.9m).

Two fenders are needed here to bring the protection out beyond the back of the rudder.

The workhorses of the modern canal system, the humble work flat normally has one cabin but this one has two. They are unpowered and are either taken to the location required by a tug or fitted with an outboard engine. They provide a mobile workshop for maintenance work on the canal system.

A flight of locks was required where a canal had to climb up (or down) a steep hill.

Flight A series of locks one after another with a 'pound' in between to allow craft to pass each other. A staircase is a flight of locks where you pass straight from one lock to the next (*see* Staircase). Flights and staircases are how canals climb up (or down) a hill.

Fly boats High-speed craft that used to 'fly' non-stop to their destination, often with up to four crews, one asleep or at rest and the others working the boat. Some had a large knife arrangement at the fore end to slice through the tow ropes of any boats who did not clear a path for them.

Footings The bottom part of the side of a boat (*see* Craft Sides).

Freeboard The distance from the gunwhale to the waterline. Of course, on a working boat this would have been less when the boat was loaded than when empty. This does not often change on a modern private pleasure or residential craft.

Gas *See* LPG.

Gunwale Deck of a narrow boat at the top of the side of the craft, normally 3–4in (8–10cm) wide, to which the cloths were attached.

Headlight Boats are required to have a headlight or 'tunnel light', so called as it produces a diffused light that provides illumination in a tunnel without blinding the crew of any boat coming toward you. Some craft today have twin halogen spot lights that do just that. Whilst headlights are used for operating after dark, the idea is to show where you are in a tunnel rather than to see with.

Hold The part of the boat that was filled with cargo. As with any commercial carrying craft, the hold took up most of a narrow boat. Bulk cargo, such as coal, was simply poured in and was then shovelled out on arrival at its destination. For other cargo, the hold would be sheeted in with cloths on an A frame formed by the top plank, which rested on the box masts positioned down the centre of the boat, the deck board at the fore end and the cabin block on the roof of the engine room at the stern. The living space on a modern narrow boat is still sometimes referred to as the hold.

This narrow boat is still in commercial use. This shot was taken after the craft had been emptied of the ballast for a docking and the shuts have been removed so you can see the keelson, bottom planks and the internal structure of the hull. The mast, top planks, stands and the cratch still need to be removed.

A Joey boat in the out-of-use lock at the top of Stoke Bruerne flight.

Hold back To slow or stop a craft to allow another craft to complete a manoeuvre, for example, to come through a bridge.

Ice In cold weather the surface of a canal can be covered in ice, which can be a hazard. If a narrow boat 'punches' the ice the friction will, over time, thin the plate at the front of the craft. It has also happened that a narrow boat can cause a slice of ice to break off and skim over the surface of the ice and cut into the hull of a moored GRP cruiser – this is rare but care should be taken when navigating through an ice-covered canal. Thick ice on the surface can also result in loss of directional control of the craft.

Inverter A unit that converts low-voltage DC current (12v or 24v) to mains AC current (230v or 240v) to enable mains equipment to be used from the boat's batteries.

Joey An open day boat used mainly on the BCN (Birmingham Canal Navigations). The rudder could be lifted off from one end and put on the other, which saved taking the boat to a 'winding hole' or turning point. They were, in the main, used for short-haul cargo trips. *See also* Station boat.

Joshers Distinctively well-made boats built for Fellows, Morton and Clayton named after the man who designed them, Joshua Fellows. He was the son of the founder of the company, James. FMC owned one of the largest fleets on the inland waterways and in the early 1900s had the largest fleet of steam-powered narrow boats on the system, many of which still exist.

Joshers, named after Joshua Fellows, were considered by some as the Rolls Royces of carrying craft.

GLOSSARY

This is a Humber keel, still in commercial use, carrying coal.

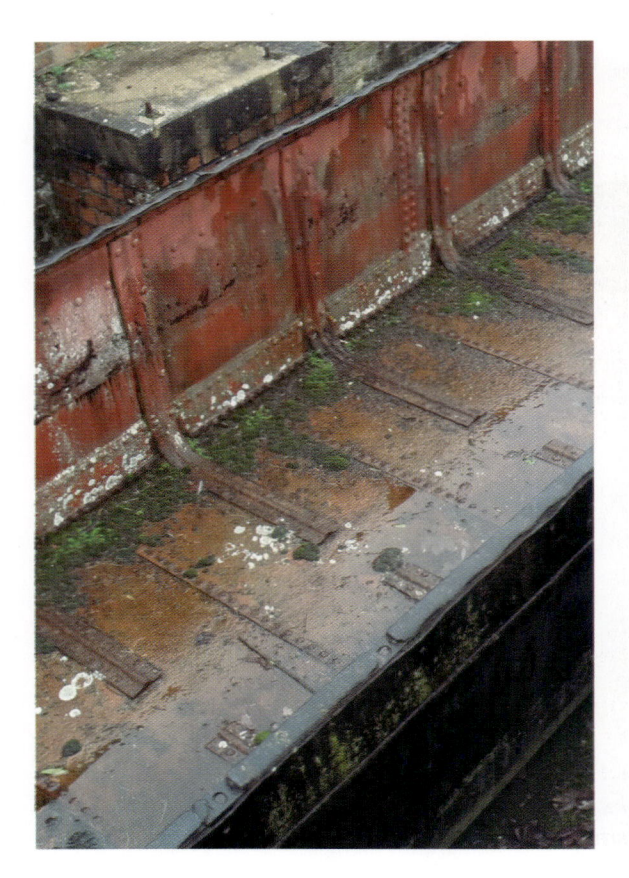

Keel (craft) An inland barge from the northeast of England, found on the Humber, Trent, Yorkshire Ouse and connecting waterways. There were also Humber sloops. Humber keels have outlived many of the other types and can still be found in commercial use on the waterways of the Northeast. Many have found their way south and have been converted to other uses, such as houseboats, hotels and trip boats. The South had Thames Barges, the Midlands wherries and on the River Severn trows; there is only one trow left (at present understood to be at Ironbridge) and a handful, if any, wherries. All these barges were built primarily for cargo carrying on the inland waterways but could be taken to sea.

Knees Knees or ribs are L-shaped sections that hold the sides of the craft in place and also connect the sides and bottom, thus contributing to the integ-

The knees of a craft connect the sides to the bottom. This boat is in the disused lock at Stoke Bruerne and is part of the museum.

rity of the whole hull. They are used in both steel (or iron) and wooden craft and can themselves be made of wood or metal, but wooden knees are much larger than iron or steel ones in order to provide the necessary strength. In wooden craft they are connected with large coach bolts, and in steel and iron craft by rivets and later by welding.

Lace plates See Ribbon Plates.

LASH See BACAT.

Leggers Gangs of men who were hired to 'walk' a boat through a tunnel where there was no towpath for the horse. Planks (wings) were put out from the boat and the men would lie on these planks and walk along the tunnel wall. Legging can also be undertaken lying on your back and walking along the tunnel roof. The horse meanwhile was taken over the hill. At first, it was the boat crew who legged the boat through, but later gangs of men were licensed for this by the canal company. Steam tugs, and later diesel engines, made the practice obsolete. You can try out legging on certain days in Dudley Tunnel at the Black Country Museum.

Lighter A craft used to 'lighten' a ship and carry the cargo further upstream. Such craft were normally unpowered and towed in trains by a tug. In effect these were barges. Many today have been turned into houseboats, and some have been put into commercial use as office space and bars. On the canal system such craft were built for maintenance use.

Lighters come in all shapes and sizes. This is a maintenance lighter used for the removal of dredging and other similar work on the canal system, such as carrying piling. Cargo lighters, used to transfer goods from ships further inland, would have been bigger but the size of locks would have been a deciding factor.

GLOSSARY

Lock The structure used to get craft from one level of waterway to another. The first locks were 'flash' locks built into a weir. These were wasteful in both time and water as they only had one gate separating the upper and lower reach. The pound lock, with mitre gates at either end, lets the craft go up or down in the chamber between the two sets of gates. Water is let into or out of a lock by winding up paddles with a windlass at one end of the lock. Once the level is made, the gates can be opened for the craft to enter/leave the lock. *See also* Paddle Gear.

Many locks on the main lines of the canal system are wide locks, able to take a pair of narrow boats side by side.

Image of a lock showing the towpath on the left with a horse ramp.

Lock key See Paddle Gear, Windlass.

Long line See Rope.

LPG (liquid petroleum gas) Most boats use gas to power a number of appliances, including cookers, fridges, water heaters and (not so often these days) lighting. Gas heaters, however, are not a good idea on a boat as the amount of gas burnt releases a large amount of water into the atmosphere on the craft. Movable gas heaters on wheels are not allowed. Gas cylinders are required to be stored in a gas-tight locker that vents overboard. LPG generally comes in two types of cylinders, red and blue (propane and butane respectively), although some companies use other colours. Most boats use propane, as butane can freeze in winter. Some say butane is safer but any gas can be dangerous. Gas should always be fitted by a Gas Safe-registered fitter.

Masts Narrow boats do have a mast – at least the old working boats had. They were used, together with two stands, to support the top plank that ran from the cratch to the cabin block on the roof of the engine room and which in turn provided support for the cloths (or tarpaulins) used to cover the goods in the hold in wet weather. It was normal practice to run down the top plank to get from one end of the boat to the other. Modern narrow boats, of course, do not have these or need them – they have a 'lid', or superstructure, over the hold.

This shot shows the layout of the hold and the location of the mast and stands. A top plank would be run along the top of these from the cratch to the cabin top and from this would be hung the cloths or tarpaulins to protect the cargo.

Mooring pin Device like a very large nail that can be banged into the towpath for the crew of a boat to tie up to, either overnight or for a longer period. If the crew are lucky, they will find rings (mooring rings) embedded into the towpath which they can tie to instead, which will save having to hammer the pin in and get the pin out again. In modern times, a number of devices have appeared that slip into the connecting strip of the campshedding along the side of the canal, some being more effective than others. The most successful is a length of chain with two large loops at each end, one of which will slip through the other. A mooring pin can be a trip hazard on the towpath at night and most boat owners tie some white material to the top of the pin to make it easier for those walking on the towpath to see it. *See also* Bollards, Rings.

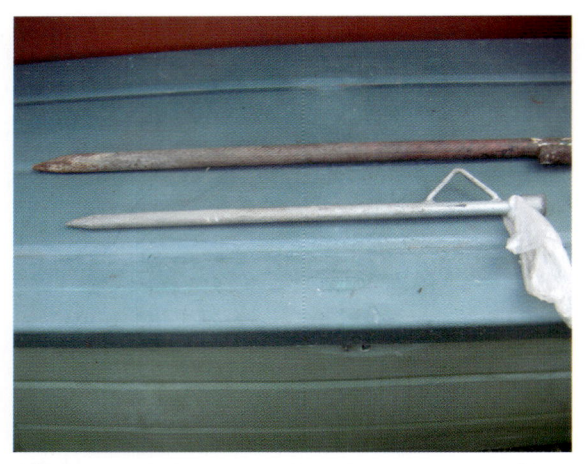

A mooring pin is inserted into the bank using either a club hammer or a sledge hammer.

Morse control Unofficial name for a single lever control (Morse was the name of a maker), which enables the steerer to change speed and direction of the propeller with one lever. Traditional narrow boats had two levers – a gear lever with three posi-

Although you cannot see the ropes – which would have been in an X shape from the stern of the motor to the bow of the butty – you can see how close the craft are: care needs to be taken when slowing down to avoid the butty hitting the stern of the motor boat

GLOSSARY

This boat is fitted with a Morse control, which is located inside the back doors.

tions (forward, reverse and neutral) and a speed wheel to control the speed of the engine.

Motor A narrow boat with an engine. Narrow boats used to travel in pairs, with a motor towing a butty on a long line (or snubber), breasted up (tied side by side) or on cross straps (with the nose of the butty hard against the stern of the motor).

Motor butty A butty that has been motorized. This normally involves fitting an inboard engine but one or two are powered with an outboard engine, connected either to the rudder or to the side of the craft. The latter makes the craft much more difficult to steer and is not recommended. There are also examples of hydraulic drives being fitted. A motor butty can often be identified as such, as it is normal to leave the butty tiller/rudder in place and these were much larger than required on a motor to enable a bigger 'bite' on the water flow.

Mud box A filter on raw water cooling systems to stop mud and other unwanted particles, such as weed, being drawn into the water cooling system, thus blocking it and resulting in the overheating of the engine.

Mud weight A metal weight tied to the craft where it was not possible to tie to land. Often a 56lb (25kg) weight was used and dropped into the silt at the bottom of the canal instead of an anchor.

Mud weights are 56lb weights used to hold one end of a boat in place where it has to stick out from the wharf, towpath or bank. They are also handy as ballast.

Narrow boat A goods-carrying craft designed over 200 years ago, which, due to the size of the locks on the Midlands canal system, was 71ft 6in by 7ft beam (21.8m by 2.1m). The original craft were horse-drawn but later they were motorized, first with steam engines, then semi-diesel and finally normal diesel engines, usually with two or three cylinders. It was found that a motor boat would have enough power to tow another craft behind it. These were originally old horse-drawn craft but later purpose-made 'butty' boats were built; a motor boat could carry about 25 tons and tow a butty that could carry 30 tons. Two boats were easier to handle than one barge and so narrow boats working in pairs were favoured, which also provided the option of navigating on the narrow canals, where a barge would have had to transfer the cargo into a pair of narrow boats for onward shipment.

GLOSSARY

A pair of boats – a motor and a butty – working breasted up. This slows the unit down but is easier to steer. This system would be used where the locks were close to each other.

Narrow boat pair A pair of boats – motor boat and a butty or unpowered boat – working together. The pair would breast up in a 14ft-wide (4.2m) lock but in single locks (7ft/2.1m wide) the motor would go first and then the butty would be manhandled through.

No. 1s Owner boatmen who only had one craft in their fleet (some had butties but these were not called No. 2s!). While most of the narrow boats on the system were part of large fleets, there was a considerable number of private craft used for general goods-carrying.

Packet boat Craft used to carry mail, small parcels and passengers.

Paddle gear The equipment used to let water into or out of a lock, set either on the gate (gate paddle) or in the ground by the gate (ground paddle). The paddle is set into a windlass, which is raised or lowered using a windlass handle (windlass or handle for short but *not* lock key). There were also side paddles, which let the water into or out of a side pond, but most of these have now been removed. Lock keys are allen keys used to unlock the paddle gear and are used to prevent vandalism. They are found in locations where this has presented a problem to the navigation authority in the past. The most common cause of accidents on the canal system is people leaving a windlass on the paddle. If the paddle drops, which can happen for a number of reasons, the windlass can fly round at high speed and can cause injury to any bystander. When the boat is in the lock, paddles should be raised slowly, as raising them too fast will cause turbulence in the lock and slam the boat into the gates. *See also* Windlass.

GLOSSARY 137

This is a ground paddle and allows the lock to fill up from the top pound through a channel in the lock brickwork. If the paddle is raised too quickly in a wide lock, it will cause the bow of the craft to be pushed sideways with some force.

The propeller of a boat provides the powerhouse of the craft. The engine is connected to the propeller via a gearbox through the hull at the back of the boat. The propeller sucks water from in front of the craft and pushes it over the rudder, which, if turned, will alter the direction of the flow and thus the direction of the craft.

Polystyrene insulation In the 1960s and 70s a very cheap form of insulation used in narrow boats and barges was ceiling tiles made of expanded polystyrene. These were a great fire risk, however, and few boats are now insulated in this way. Modern boats are sometimes insulated using spray foam. This is also a type of polystyrene but is fire retardant and has the advantage of getting into all the corners.

Pound The stretch of water between two locks. On the Thames, this is called a reach. A pound lock is a lock with two gates and a lock chamber in between that will take one or more craft. A single-gate lock was called a flash lock, but there are none of these left! *See* Locks.

Propeller Mechanical device for moving a boat by turning rotational motion into thrust. The modern propeller is based on an idea of I. K. Brunel when he designed his iron steamship *SS Great Britain*, now a museum in Bristol Floating Harbour. The success of this design resulted in most craft being fitted with a propeller of this type rather than paddle wheels. The modern propeller fitted to a barge or narrow boat is normally three-bladed and is located at the end of the swim. It is attached to a propeller shaft, which enters the craft through the stern tube and is then connected to the engine via a gearbox. To stop the propeller flying off, it is held in place with a nut, which in turn is kept in position with a split pin. The split pin needs to be inspected on a regular basis and replaced if required.

Puddling clay A mixture of clay and water used to line a canal to keep it watertight. At wharves the edge of the canal is brick-lined.

Push tug A type of tug that can either tow another craft (or train of craft) from in front (the normal way) or push from the rear. The connection between the tug and the tow has to be firm – often made with steel ropes tied tightly to prevent sway. Some modern tugs are fitted to enable both towing from the front of the craft or pushing from behind.

GLOSSARY

Railways The canal engineers laid out the route of a waterway by the most level course, and later the engineers laying our railway network followed the same route. As a result, many railways run alongside or across a canal. In the mid-1960s many such lines were closed so there are also a large number of railway overbridges, some of which have had the decking removed.

Ram's head Decorative rope arrangement around the top of the rudder on a butty.

Recreational Craft Directive (RCD) Specification of the EU standards for craft construction that came into force in all EU states in June 1998. It has since been updated at least twice. These standards will still apply after the UK leaves the EU, as craft from the UK are sold in both the EU and the UK, and UK residents may want to take their craft to the EU.

Registered vessel A registration number is issued by the navigation authorities but, like a car number plate, it does not provide evidence of ownership. A very small number of narrow boats and a larger (but still small percentage) of barges are registered with the Small Ships Register. This confirms ownership and also enables a marine mortgage to be raised on the craft as opposed to a personal loan, which is limited to ten years. Craft have been sold on without altering the SSR registration, which leaves the original owner still being the legal owner. The SSR name may also differ from the name carried on the craft, which would add to the confusion.

Ribbon plates A popular decorative item, also called a lace plate, in back cabins in the 1800s. The plates had ribbon laced through holes in the edges and a picture in the middle, typically of fruit or animals or a seaside town with the inscription

On the canal network you will often encounter the remains of long-abandoned railways. Some have been turned into footpaths and a few have been converted into roads. Many have had the bridges removed but the abutments left behind.

Lace or ribbon plates were used to decorate the back cabins of working narrow boats. This tradition has continued to the modern day, with boat owners still collecting and displaying lace plates on their craft.

Mooring rings are used for medium- and long-term mooring of craft.

Rope should always be kept handy ready for use at both ends of the boat. At the stern it should not be kept on the counter stern, where it can be knocked over the side and foul the propeller. It should also not be kept on the tiller pin for the same reason (and you also risk the loss of the tiller pin).

'Present from …'. In the 1970s and 80s you could pick up a lace plate in an antique shop for a couple of pounds. Prices went up to an average of £30 but have since fallen again. A brass version, called a butterfly plate, was also made, but there were not so many of these.

Ribs *See* Knees. (RIB is also the acronym for Rigid Inflatable Boat. These are not often found on the canal system.)

Rings Metal hoops embedded into the wharf or towpath to enable a craft to tie up without hammering in a mooring pin.

Rope Rope has different names depending on the craft it is used on and where that craft is used. On the canal we have snubbers, 70ft (21m) lines used for towing (otherwise called a long line); straps that are 30–40ft (9–12m) long used for tying up, throwing and holding on to bollards; and cross straps, which are about 6ft (2m) long and used for breasting up or close towing (hence the term – two straps cross over each other from the dollies on the rear of the motor and the T stud on the butty, forming an X). One length should never be used for this, as the strap will ride the T stud, leading to loss of steering.

Scumbling or graining A painting system used on narrow boats to imitate wood-grain effect. It is produced by painting the surface to be covered with a cream paint, which, once dry, is then covered with dark paste mixed with oil. The area is then combed through with rubber combs, allowing the cream to show through in some parts and leaving deep varnish furrows in others.

Semi-diesel The first diesel engines used on narrow boats. Most were 9 or 15hp single-cylinder engines built by Bolinder, although there were other makes. They were 'heavy oil' engines, which were started by heating a special bulb with a blow lamp and then kicking the flywheel.

Shaft A long pole used to push the craft out if the wind prevents the steerer from doing so from the stern, or for pushing the bow out if the craft becomes 'stemmed up' (runs aground). A shorter version with a hook at one end, called a cabin shaft, was kept on the roof at the stern. The word 'shaft' is also used to describe the prop shaft between the engine and propeller.

Short boat Northern version of the narrow boat. These were shorter and wider (62ft by up to 14ft 6in, or 18.9m by 4.4m) and were designed to fit the locks on the northern canals. Although they are of similar construction to southern boats, their heavier weight requires a higher third-party element to the insurance premium and barge rates should be used.

A narrow boat door showing traditional painting designs surrounded by a scumbled border.

Kennet *at Ellesmere Port in restored condition.*

Side pound Chambers fitted next to many locks that were used to save water. In the days of the British Waterways Board most of these were allowed to fall into disrepair and few, if any, are now in use although the evidence of their existence is often still there. The idea was, when going downhill, to let the water out of a lock into the chamber at the side of the lock (often there were two at different levels), rather than out of the bottom of the lock and on down the canal. A boat going uphill would then fill the lock from the side pound first rather than taking the water from the level above.

Skeg A connection running underneath the propeller between the bottom of the rudder housing and the counter that supports the bottom of the rudder. This can become bent if the craft is grounded or 'cills' in a lock.

Snatch Inland waterway term for a tow. To 'snatch off' is to pull a boat off a shallow/sandbank (known as being 'stemmed up'). This assistance is often given by one boat to another on the inland system and is covered under an insurance policy as normal canal practice, as long as this is done simply to assist the other boat owner and no fee is involved. *See also* Towing.

Snatcher A short snubber (rope) for towing under certain conditions, such as in short pounds. It is 40–50ft (12–15m) in length.

Snubber *See* Rope.

Spring A method of tying up a boat with lines tied in both directions (that is, one pointing forward and one aft) from the anchor point on the boat, which prevents movement of the craft caused by passing craft travelling at too high a speed.

Springer A type of modern steel canal cruiser built by Sam Springer. The original Springers were built of steel recovered from demolished gas holders.

Staircase A series of locks where the top gate of one lock forms the bottom gate of the next. As there is no facility for craft to pass each other on a staircase, you have to make sure the locks are not in use before starting up/down.

A staircase is a flight of locks with one lock leading straight into the next. With no pound in between, there is no place to pass other craft in the narrow flight.

Station boat Similar to a Joey but a craft owned by a railway company (most by the LMS but some by the GWR, regional rail companies prior to the formation of British Railways) and used on the BCN (Birmingham Canal Navigation) in the same way – to reach the factories that were on the vast BCN network from the railway depots. They were built by Yarwoods, who also contributed to the GUCC fleet.

Stem up To run aground. In the 1960s and 70s this was an event that could happen several times in a trip but as the British Waterways Board improved the depth of the system, it is not such a common problem on most of the system today, although it can still happen. Dredging is not so common today as it once was. On rivers, sand banks and shallows

Here you can see the back of the boat, with the propeller connected to the shaft and under this the skeg, which protects the propeller and supports the rudder. You can also clearly see the sacrificial chine.

A boat that was once owned by the Great Western Railway with an LMS boat behind.

cause the same problem. The normal way to free the craft is to rock it from side to side with the engine in slow reverse gear. The boat should slide back the way it came!

Stern gear The rudder, propeller and prop shaft assembly at the back (stern) of the boat. The rear of any powered narrow boat or barge is laid out in very much the same way. The back of the boat tapers underwater to the point where the propeller sits on the end of the prop shaft, which comes out of the boat through the stern tube. The propeller is under the counter, which on a modern boat will have a weed hatch in it to allow easy clearing of any rubbish caught around the prop and stern gear. The water is sucked along this taper and pushed out by the propeller onto the rudder. A locking nut with a split pin keeps the prop on the shaft. The rudder is connected to the tiller or steering wheel. *See also* Swim and Stern tube.

Stern tube The outlet through the hull that carries the propeller shaft from the gearbox and engine to the propeller. Because the engine and gearbox are inside the craft and the propeller is outside, the stern tube has to be watertight and this is achieved by thoroughly coating it in water-resistant grease, which is pumped in from a greaser. Failure to keep the stern tube greased will result in water gaining access to the hull so it is essential to top up the seal after the engine has been run.

Stop lock A type of lock designed to completely stop the flow of water. Such locks were originally built at junctions between different company's waterways. The idea was to conserve water for one company or another when the waterway was not in use. Tolls were often charged at a stop lock. Single-gate stop locks are often installed in long stretches of canal to be shut in the event of a breach to save water and to maintain levels.

The stop lock at Paddington in London. Stop locks were installed for one of two reasons: to stop a canal taking the water supply from another company, or to protect a stretch of water where there was danger of a breach (often one set of gates was used in such locations).

GLOSSARY

Stop planks A simple alternative to a single gate, these are thick planks that fit into slots on either side of the canal, normally at a bridge hole or at a special narrowing put in for the purpose. This allows the water to be removed prior to maintenance work being undertaken. Stop planks can also be used in the same way as a stop lock to prevent water loss in the event of a breach. Sites for stop planks can be found all over the canal system at locations such as embankments, aqueducts and so on. The planks will often be found in small brick or concrete structures close to the site. They can also be fitted at either end of locks to enable the lock to be drained for maintenance work.

Stoppage Closure or partial closure of the canal. There two types of stoppages: planned ones for maintenance work, and emergency ones caused by a problem with the waterway (such as a breach or damage to a lock). A list of planned stoppages can be obtained from CRT or EA each year. A lock on a flight can be damaged, requiring repairs, and thus a sudden stoppage can be caused because craft are unable to use the lock until the repairs have been carried out.

Summit pound Where the waterway reaches the top of a hill. Canal companies have always had problems supplying water to these top levels and resorted to all sorts of methods to keep the level of the water up. Most, if not all, summit pounds are fed by reservoirs, and are often kept full by pumping engines. Another way of keeping the canal full is by 'back pumping', which as the name suggests, involves pumping water back up a flight of locks. The pumps were steam driven at the start but later became diesel and then electric.

Swim The rear of the boat tapers towards the back so that water flows onto the propeller to provide forward motion and then onto the rudder to give direction. This taper is called the swim, and the longer the swim the better. A short swim can cause greater wash (*see* Wash).

The slots into which stop planks are fitted at the head of a lock to allow maintenance.

This side shot shows the swim, which tapers to the propeller under the counter. The longer the swim, the faster you can go without creating wash.

GLOSSARY 145

Tiller An S-shaped piece of metal connected to the rudder to enable a craft to be steered. Tiller steering is used on 98 per cent of narrow boats and a large percentage of barges. This is an alternative to a steering wheel, which can be found on many types of craft, but provides an easier way to handle a narrow boat.

Photo showing the tiller bar in the swan's neck and the tiller pin connecting the two.

A tiller pin keeps the tiller from falling off the swan's neck. While a screwdriver would do the job, it is common practice to have an ornate brass top. This one is a kingfisher but there are hundreds of designs to choose from.

Tiller pin Normally, on a narrow boat, a brass top on a steel shaft that fits into a hole through both the tiller and the top of the swan's neck holding the tiller in position. It can be pulled so that the tiller can be removed when the craft is tied up.

Originally made of steel, it is thought that a boater once fitted a brass ball to the top of his pin for decoration, and this was copied on other boats. There are now many nice little brass decorative tiller pins on the market. These are not traditional but many boat owners have adopted such pins over the last thirty years, and one company, Draco Crafts, will make them to order.

Some boat owners cast quite ornate pins as a hobby and make them available to fellow boaters.

Tom pudding or pan Craft designed for the waterways of the Northeast to carry coal. They were in fact boxes which were formed into trains and then had a false bow (called a jebus) and stern fitted before being taken down the waterway. The train could be longer than the locks, in which case it would have to be split to work through. At the end of the trip the train was split up into individual units, which were picked up and emptied into ships or railway wagons using a wheel-type arrangement.

Top plank Plank on a carrying narrow boat that runs from the front of the engine room cabin to the cratch, supported by masts. It can, of course, be removed. It is wide enough to run down but was mainly used to support the covers or cloths that were draped over it in tent shape and secured to the gunwales. These were fitted to protect the cargo from wet weather and theft.

Towing Pulling a boat along by external agency, usually horse or another boat. Regular towing of craft is as old as the canal system itself. Before engines, all craft were towed by horses and other animals. With the introduction of powered craft, it became normal practice for one powered craft to tow a second one, and where the canal had wide locks, the two could go through side by side. Where the canal was equipped with single locks the motor was taken through first and the butty had to be manhandled through afterwards. Today, towing of one craft by another is normal and customary on the inland waterways and is acceptable subject to no money changing hands (see also Tugs).

Towpath Path that runs beside the canal down the entire length of the waterway. It was originally called the towing path because it was used by the horses who towed the boats before engines were fitted. On the offside of the canal there is normally (but not always) a smaller strip of land known as a malice strip. This was originally owned by the canal company for maintenance. The towpath is today no longer used for the original purpose, but mainly for leisure activities such as fishing, walking and cycling. It also often offers a convenient route to lay fibre-optic cables and other service lines.

Working boats moored up. The nearest one, Jaguar, has its top plank in place.

GLOSSARY 147

A motor boat towing a butty on a long line. This was the best way to tow where there was a greater distance between locks but took greater skill when slowing or stopping, for example to enter a lock.

A typical scene on a canal towpath. Towpaths are used by walkers, anglers and cyclists.

There are many designs of tug boats on the inland waterways but the largest fleet is represented by this tug in BWB blue livery. This version can tow from the front of the craft being towed or can be used as a pusher tug.

Tug Craft used to shunt other craft in basins, tow craft through tunnels and also to tow unpowered craft round unlocked (or low locked) parts of the system, such as the BCN. The term also describes the use to which the craft is put. Tugs are still built today for both commercial and private pleasure use. Many maintenance craft are dumb (not fitted with an engine), as they often stay in the same place for long periods so having an engine installed would be a waste.

Tumblehome The inner slope of the cabin profile. The cabin narrows from gunwales to roof to protect it from damage when going through tunnels and bridges.

T stud A stud at the fore end of a craft, usually in the shape of a T, for tying a rope to. This would be used for tying up or when the craft is being towed.

Tunnel Where the canal passes through a hill. There are a number of tunnels on the canal system, all of varying lengths. Some are quite short and others really long, taking an hour or more to pass through; in most cases, you can see the end of the tunnel. Many do not have towpaths. When navigat-

GLOSSARY 149

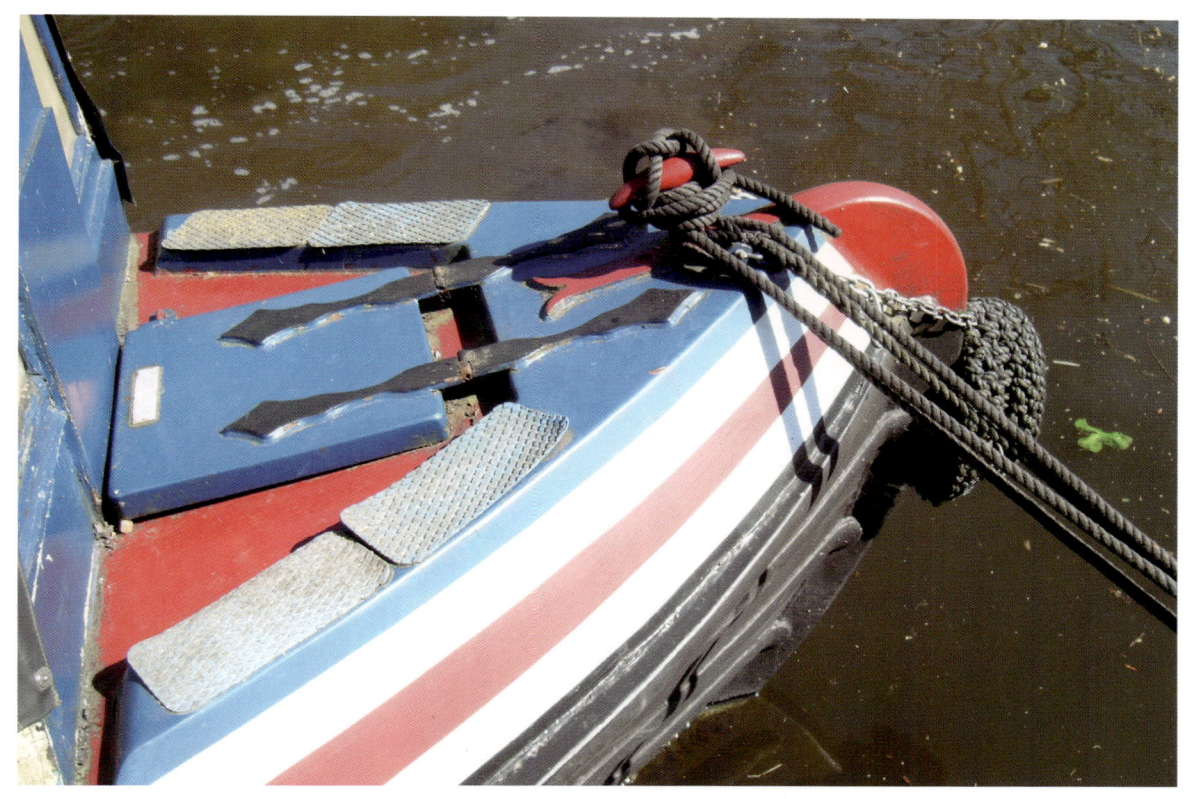

A T stud at the front of the boat is used to tie a rope to when mooring up or being towed by another craft.

Tunnels can get very wet as water seeps through the lining and can soak the crew of a boat passing underneath.

ing through a tunnel, a craft must carry a tunnel lamp. This is a white light on the cratch or on the bow. It is intended to show your craft to other boats, not to blind the crew of a boat coming the other way.

Owners of wide-beam craft should report to the local CRT office prior to entering most tunnels to arrange one-way working, as craft would not be able to pass inside the tunnel (Stoke Bruerne and

The entrance, or portal, to a tunnel. This one has a towpath but most do not.

GLOSSARY 151

Turnover bridges were provided where the towpath changed sides so that a horse could cross without unhitching the tow rope.

Blisworth are examples). In the days of horse-drawn boats, the horse would be taken over the hill and gangs of leggers would be hired to 'walk' the boat through the tunnel (*see* Leggers).

Tunnel light   *See* headlight.

Turnover bridge   A bridge designed to allow a horse to cross the canal while towing a boat without the need to unhitch the horse from the boat (also called a roving bridge). Such bridges either had spiral ramps leading up each side of the bridge, or were cantilevered, with a slot in the middle for the tow rope to pass through.

Uxter plate   The underside of the counter at the stern of a boat.

Warehouse   Buildings for storage of goods unloaded from craft or waiting to be loaded onto craft.

This picture shows the base of the turnover bridge and the path the horse would take.

There are many examples of such buildings throughout the canal system, many of which have found new uses as business premises or clubhouses. Some were quite small, while others were several storeys high, such as those at Gloucester Docks.

Wash (from a craft) As a craft passes through water under power, a wave comes out from the stern caused by the action of the propeller and the shape of the craft. This produces a wave effect known as wash. The height and power of the wash is determined by a number of factors, such as the speed of the craft, the shape of the hull, the size and speed of the propeller and the depth of the water. On a shallow canal it is easier to throw up a wash and so the craft will have to maintain a lower speed.

Washer Josher A name given to a modern craft built in the style of a Josher and using washers welded on in the place of rivets to make it look like a riveted craft – quite effective if viewed from a distance. *See* Josher.

The canal system was designed and built for the transportation of goods, and warehouses were built across the country to provide temporary storage of goods in transit.

Warehouses come in all sizes, from the very small at a local country wharf to massive five- or six-storey buildings in city centres. This is an example of a smaller, two-storey structure.

GLOSSARY 155

While very handy if your propeller gets fouled, a weed hatch can be the cause of sinking the craft if care is not taken. It should not only be secure while the craft in in gear but should also comply with the BSS in respect of height above the normal water level of the craft.

Weak link   A link in a chain that is weaker than the others, so will snap if the chain comes under pressure. This can be achieved by cutting through a link in the chain with a hacksaw, or replacing one of the links with a piece of twine. It is wise to have a weak link in the chains that attach the fenders to your boat in case a fender is caught in a lock gate – it's far better to loose a fender than sink your boat.

Weed hatch   A steel plate bolted over a hole in the hull above the propeller, which, when opened, allows access to the back of the propeller and prop shaft to enable you to clear rubbish from the area. Ex-working craft did not have a weed hatch, so if you were 'propped up' (something was caught around the prop that either slowed it down or stopped it turning completely), you had to fiddle with a boat hook to clear the obstruction. Modern craft are fitted with a weed hatch. The hole is raised above the waterline, so a baffle plate is also fitted to give the counter plate a solid surface. The quickest way to sink a narrow boat is to run the engine in gear with the weed hatch open. Always make sure that the engine is turned off before you open the weed hatch and that the hatch cover is correctly installed and bolted back down before starting the engine again.

Winding/winding hole   Turning a boat around on the canal. The term comes from the fact that you use the wind to help turn the craft. As the canal is not wide enough to turn a boat around there are points along the waterway where a bay (winding hole) on the opposite side from the towpath allows craft to be turned (some of these can be found on the towpath side). Fishing and mooring are not allowed opposite or in a winding hole. You would normally put the bow into the winding hole to avoid fouling the propeller on underwater junk dropped in by passers-by – a mattress round the prop can take hours to cut off. You then use the motor to move the back of the boat gently round, then, when it is in the correct position, reverse, pulling the boat back into the channel. You can, of course, also turn round at a junction or any other point where the waterway is wide enough.

Along the canal system there are special places to enable a full length boat to be turned, called winding holes. This one is below the last lock at Uxbridge by the Malt Shovel pub.

GLOSSARY 157

GLOSSARY

Windlass An L-shaped handle (proper name windlass handle) with a square spindle at one end which is used to raise the ratchet that draws up the paddle in the gate or by the side of a gate at a lock. The ratchet is connected to the paddle. In the up position, the paddle opens access for water to go into or out of a lock chamber. This enables a craft to be raised or lowered in a lock. The term 'lock key' is often used but is the wrong term for this item! A lock key is used to unlock the paddle gear so that the windlass handle can be used, thus preventing vandalism. Today there are many different types, from steel to gunmetal. The best modern windlasses are made of aluminium and have one tapered hole that fits all paddle gear. *See also* Paddle gear.

Wings Boards that were placed out from the bows of the craft for the leggers to lie on to walk the craft through a tunnel. *See also* Leggers.

Work flat *See* Flat.

The windlass (handle) is used to operate the paddle gear at locks.

INDEX

alarms   70, 105
anchors   65, 105

barges   19, 109
bath   63
batteries   72
Boat Safety Scheme   52, 110
Bolinder   13
bow thruster   79, 110
breaking down   83
breasting up   66, 112
Bridgewater Canal   37
Buckby cans   62, 114
butties   9, 14, 115

carbon monoxide   89
commercial craft   29, 119
condensation   54
continental waterways   104
cooking   68
craft layout   20
cratch   24, 120
cross straps   66 see also rope
cruisers   16
cut   35, 121
cutter   21,22, 122

deck board   24 see also cratch
dry dock   55

electricity   70
engines   75
engine controls   80

fenders   65, 125

fire   88
fire fighting   69
fuel tank   81

gas (LPG)   68 see also LPG
generator storage   74
Glass Reinforced Plastic (GRP)   16

heating   67
heavy oil engines   29
horn   66
houseboats   20

Inland Waterways Association   34, 38
insurance   50

layout (craft)   20
licence   49
lock handles (Windlass handles)   65
locks   8, 94, 132
LPG (gas)   68, 133

mains power   73
maintenance   50
moorings   49
mooring up   91
museums   101

narrow boat   11, 135
navigations   35

osmosis   17

painting   58
plumbing   63

pumps   63

residential craft   32
River & Canal Rescue   83
rivers   35
ropes   92, 139
roses and castles   59

scumbling   60, 140
shared ownership   47
short boat   17, 140
shower   63
signwriting   61
sinking   84
sound signals   96
snubber   66 *see also* rope
speeding   91
staircase (locks)   38, 141
steam   13

steam engines   29
straps   66
surveys   52

television   71
toilets   63
tools   83
top plank   25, 146

voltage   72

water cans   62
water heater   63
water ingress   55
Waterway Recovery Group   34, 36
wet dock   56
windlass   65, 156
winterising   51